Psychic Power

DISCOVER AND DEVELOP
YOUR SIXTH SENSE AT ANY AGE

Rob MacGregor

Foreword by Joe McMoneagle
Remote Reviewer #001
Project Stargate

BARRON'S

To Trish and Megan, wife and daughter
and fellow explorers

Many thanks to Joe and Scooter

"We should develop these abilities because it is possible for us to do so, and because doing so will enrich our lives."

The Mind Race, by Russell Targ and Keith Harary, 1984

"But now we discover what poets and mystics have always suspected: Our minds are star-gates, our bodies celled of mysteries; what was taken to be remote is actually our near neighbor in the all-reaching compass of the mind."

—Jean Houston, 2005

All inquiries should be addressed to:
Barron's Educational Series, Inc.
250 Wireless Boulevard
Hauppauge, New York 11788
www.barronseduc.com

ISBN-13: 978-0-7641-7887-0
ISBN-10: 0-7641-7887-3

Library of Congress Catalog Card No. 2004055076

Library of Congress Cataloging-in-Publication Data

MacGregor, Rob.
    Psychic power : discover and develop your sixth sense at any
age / Rob MacGregor.
        p. cm.
    ISBN 0-7641-7887-3
        1. Psychic ability.   I. Title

BF1031.M3416 2005
133.8—dc22
                                                          2004055076

Printed in Canada
9 8 7 6 5 4 3 2 1

Contents

Foreword

At some point in life everyone has begun a sentence at the same time someone else did with the exact same words. Many of us have suddenly had the mental image of a friend we've not heard from for months jump into our mind's eye seconds before the phone rings, only to hear their voice at the other end of the line. And once in awhile, when we are feeling especially lucky, we'll make a quick stop to play a few dollars on those three lucky numbers that just kind of popped into our conscious thought while we sat daydreaming about our next vacation. Maybe it doesn't work all the time, but it happens enough to keep many of us betting. Why is that? Some would say it's simply coincidence; some say it's a mystery. Whatever you've thought about the world of the paranormal, it is certainly a bizarre world that usually defies explanation.

Now Rob MacGregor has done us a favor. His book *Psychic Power, Discover and Develop Your Sixth Sense at Any Age* is a virtual river of information on the strange source from which these weird and sometimes eerie powers spring—this bizarre world of the paranormal. His presentation is refreshing, up to date, non-dogmatic, and exceptionally well informed, with chapters covering the essence of what's happening right now on the paranormal fast track—the methods, techniques, exercises, and science currently in use today.

MacGregor presents real-life examples of famous psychics who have been well tested, and shares many of the techniques that will assist readers toward their own experience. He covers significant subject areas such as mind-to-mind communications, sometimes called telepathy; synchronicity; a far-seeing ability also known by the French word *clairvoyance*; psi through touch or psychometry; manipulating matter with the mind, a psychokinetic ability; the out-of-body experiences, mediumship, and some of the latest research on remote viewing, which was originally developed by scientists at Stanford

Research Institute International for use by Military Intelligence.

After having worked in the paranormal field for nearly thirty years, I can say that one thing is almost certain. Much of what one reads is either pedantic to the point of stupefying or airy to the point it becomes almost impossible to understand what the author is trying to communicate. Let's face it: It's a tough field to understand, it is an even tougher field to describe, and any-one who has ever had a bizarre or strange experience under-stands it is nearly impossible to explain. It's refreshing to see what MacGregor has done with his book. It's direct and to the point. He provides exceptional and exciting examples, practical ideas on how to channel and perfect your own skills, and where to go for more information if you need it—all up to date and well organized.

If you've never heard of the paranormal, this is the perfect book to garner a complete and basic understanding of its most recent developments. If you've had a long-time interest, MacGregor has organized a wealth of information that can add to your collection and improve your knowledge. It's a hands-on, easy-to-read desk reference that even includes an up-to-date recommended reading list for those who would like to expand into more specific areas. One might think Rob MacGregor was reading our minds when he wrote it. Read it yourself and then test your skill. You may be more psychic than you think.

Joe McMoneagle

Joseph W. McMoneagle is a retired Chief Warrant Officer, United States Army, and was Remote Viewer #001 in the Military Secret Stargate Program for 19½ years. He has authored four books on remote viewing and has had two research papers accepted for publication in scientific journals on the same subject.

Introduction

Believe it or not, you're psychic. To some extent, we all are. In fact, psychic experiences are so commonplace that many of us often don't recognize them.

For example, you start to think about a family member when someone asks about that very person. Or you get an e-mail that touches on something you were just reading about, or you think about something that is then mentioned on television or the radio. Maybe you hum a tune and suddenly the song comes on the radio. Or, you happen to think about a friend, the phone rings, and it's her. Sometimes it's the other way around. You call someone and he says, "Hey, I was just about to call you."

While such spontaneous incidents may occur frequently to you, you might not think of them as psychic experiences because you weren't trying. They just happened. But think again: Psychic power, that knack for expanding your mind beyond the five senses, takes many shapes and forms.

It also has many names. It's known as psi, pronounced "sigh." It's extrasensory perception (ESP), second sight, the sixth sense, the paranormal. It's also intuition, hunches, and insight. But let's get more specific.

Psychic power is about…

- ✪ tuning into things that haven't happened yet—that's *precognition*
- ✪ sensing what someone else is thinking—*telepathy*
- ✪ seeing what's going on elsewhere—*clairvoyance* or *remote viewing*
- ✪ moving objects with your mind—*psychokinetic energy* (PK)
- ✪ gaining information about the past through touch—*psychometry*
- ✪ experiencing meaningful coincidences—*synchronicity.*

It's also about taking control of your dreams, journeying out of body, and making contact with the spirit world. Whatever form it takes, it's all about energy and how to channel it.

With psychic power you can glimpse what's just around the corner, allowing you to prepare for or change the circumstances if you don't like the outcome. For example, for no particular reason, you decide to take a different way home, and later you hear about an accident that blocked traffic for hours on your usual route. You can find lost objects, pick up on what others are thinking, communicate telepathically with a pet, discover secrets from the past, see what's going on elsewhere, and even gain guidance from unseen helpers.

With psychic power, you gain an advantage. By getting a hint of what's going to happen, seeing what others can't see, you come out a step ahead. You glimpse a larger picture of your life. You gain higher knowledge. You use more of your brain.

Developing psychic power also can help you relax and relieve stress. Ultimately, psychic power is a window to learning more about yourself—who you are and where you're going—and making your wishes come true.

My Story

My journey into the world of psychic power began years ago, when I interviewed for a magazine article several people who called themselves professional psychics. One of them was a retired policeman who had used his abilities in his police work. In the course of the interview he told me that he saw me driving up and down the coast of Florida, where I lived, with some bulky equipment in my vehicle. He also saw me teaching a class.

Wrong and wrong, I thought. I didn't drive up and down the coast with any sort of equipment and had no plans to do any such thing. I also didn't teach or foresee myself teaching. I was a writer, not a teacher. I remember thinking that I hoped this guy was a better cop than he was a psychic.

I also interviewed a woman who worked with police in locating missing persons and solving crimes. She called herself a psychic detective and even gave seminars for police officers on how they could develop their own psychic power. Like the ex-cop, she also gave me a glimpse of my future. To my surprise, she told me I would write a book about developing psychic abilities and the book would look like a game. She also told me that I would write many books.

As it turned out, she was right on both counts. I went on to co-author a book with another psychic, Tony Grosso, whom I also interviewed for that same article. It was called *The Rainbow Oracle*, included colored cubes and a velvet pouch, and was packaged in a box. It was about developing psi talents through the use of color, and yes, it did look like a game!

Over the years, I've written more than two dozen books, both fiction and nonfiction. My most recent books include *The Complete Dream Dictionary*, *Dream Power for Teens*, and *Star Power for Teens*, an astrology book I co-authored with my teen daughter, Megan. I also wrote a yoga book, *The Lotus and the Stars: The Way of Astro-Yoga*, and *The Everything Dream Book*, both co-authored with my wife, Trish.

In addition, I've written thirteen novels, including *Prophecy Rock*, which won the Edgar Allan Poe award in the Young Adult category. My novel, *Hawk Moon*, was a finalist for the same award and was selected for the 1997 Book for the Teen Age by the New York Public Library. I'm also the author of seven Indiana Jones novels, including the adaptation of *Indiana Jones and the Last Crusade*.

As for the predictions by the ex-cop, a couple of years later, I found myself driving up and down the coast of Florida to various beaches with my bulky windsurfing gear packed in my van. I also took up yoga and became a yoga teacher, something I've now done for more than eleven years. So, as it turned out, although I had my doubts, it seems that he was right on both counts.

You Must Be Psychic

Going to a psychic, as I did, can be worthwhile. Some people are naturals. It's often an inherited trait, researchers say. But such an encounter can be expensive and sometimes an outright rip-off. However, you don't need to consult a psychic to experience psi power. You can learn to develop your own skills, and that's what this book is about.

If you're like most people, you've probably had a few psychic experiences without even trying. We're all psychic to some degree. At least, that's what some researchers tell us. "We never found anyone who couldn't learn to do it," wrote Russell Targ in *The Mind Race*, in reference to experiments in clairvoyance or remote viewing, the ability to see distant objects or events.

However, these skills have been largely neglected in our technology-oriented culture. Although you may have spontaneous psychic experiences from time to time, you probably have to *learn* how to develop your skills in order to make use of them on a regular basis. As you do so, you may encounter negative attitudes about psychic abilities from some people. But don't let their opinions deter you from your exploration. After all, what you experience and believe is more important than what they think.

Although you may have spontaneous psychic experiences from time to time, you probably have to learn how to develop your skills in order to make use of them on a regular basis.

The interesting news is that more and more people accept that extrasensory perception exists, often because they've experienced it. A Gallup poll recently asked Americans about their beliefs in a variety of psi phenomena. The results suggest a significant increase in belief in these experiences over the past decade. At least 50 percent of Americans believe in psychic or spiritual healing and extrasensory perception (ESP), and a third or more believe in such things as haunted houses and ghosts.

If my daughter and her friends are any indication, the interest among teens is even stronger. Teens who set out to develop psi power actually have an advantage over adults, who are more fully immersed in the world of logic and reasoning. While those skills are important, you gain added advantages by developing your intuitive abilities.

Whatever your age, get ready for a guided tour into the mysterious world of psi. This stuff can be complicated and confusing, but you're traveling in a friendly environment. Our journey will be safe and comfortable, but you'll also get plenty of opportunities to experience the hands-free roller coaster ride that comes along with expanding your awareness beyond its normal limits. By reading about these talents, you gain a better understanding of psi power. But to truly comprehend what it's all about, you need to experience it. So, be bold, test your abilities, and learn how to develop them as you move through the exercises in each chapter, and on the accompanying CD. The first two exercises on the CD lead you on inner journeys which help you relax, quiet your mind, and improve self-awareness. The third exercise offers an opportunity to test your ability to "see" what's taking place elsewhere and in the future.

You'll be using your imagination, enhancing your creativity, and giving yourself a chance to speculate on what's possible. Now, begin your journey into the world of psychic power.

1 The Psi in Science

You're about to embark on an exploration of the world of extrasensory perception, where the mind travels into new realms, beyond the normal way of thinking and looking at things. Albert Einstein, one of the top analytical minds of the twentieth century, attributed much of his success to a childlike sense of wonder. In fact, the theory of relativity, which showed how measurements are affected by motion and gravity, began to take shape when a sixteen-year-old Einstein imagined what it would be like to ride on a beam of light. "Imagination is more important than knowledge," he said.

No matter what your age, try to imagine this: It's your first day at a new high school in a new city where you've just moved. You're looking at the curriculum and you see a science elective that your old school didn't offer: parapsychology. In fact, you've never heard of any high school that offers the study of psychic phenomena as a subject. You start to sign up, but you're told that it's the most popular elective course and you must have all your required science courses completed and a 3.0 or better grade-point average. You qualify, you're accepted, and you get the last available seat in the class.

Now what happens? Will you be learning how to leave your body? Will you be ghost hunting or learning how to levitate small objects? On the first day of class, you get the course syllabus and find out that you're going to learn how people are tested for psychic abilities. You're also going to be conducting telepathy experiments, both as the researcher and the subject. Later, your team will get into remote viewing experiments, and you may even test your psychokinetic abilities. Before the year is over, there will be a field trip that includes an overnight stay at a haunted hotel.

You can't wait to get started. You're not only going to learn about psychic abilities, but you're going to get a chance to test your skills, and even learn how to develop these skills. Sound interesting?

Maybe someday such a class will be offered in high schools. But meanwhile, whether young or old, you can take the class right now as your own independent study course. You can do it for fun using this book and CD as your text. Take your time, study the psychic abilities that interest you, and work with the exercises. By the time you finish this course, you'll not only know a lot more about psychic power, but you'll be practicing it!

A Tale of Psychic Power

Imagine that one day a film crew from Japan shows up at your door. They've heard you're psychic and they want you to help them find a missing person. In Japan! The only information they are going to give you is the name and birth date of the missing person. But guess what? You're not even going to see it. The producer is going to seal the information in an envelope and then put a number on the envelope. The number on the envelope is all you get. Now you have to find someone on the other side of the world who has been missing for years.

Sound difficult? Not if you're Joe McMoneagle, one of the world's top remote viewers and author of four books on the topic. The less information Joe is given, the better. That's because he doesn't want to work with the left side of his brain, the area where we analyze and use logic. In other words, he doesn't want to "figure it out." Rather, he wants to use the right side of his brain, the seat of emotions and intuition. Once he quiets the internal chatter, the *pure* information comes to him as images and words. In essence, he's able to project a part of his mind to the location of the missing person, the target. So with only a number to guide him, Joe is ready to go to work. He'll focus on the number and begin "seeing" the target.

That was exactly what he did for the Japanese television crew that came to his home in Virginia on May 10, 2003, to film him as he searched for a missing person. The first clue he offered was a large Ferris wheel with changing colored lights all over it. He said he felt it was in Tokyo near water, and from the top of the Ferris wheel you could see four ball fields separated by walkways, which formed a cross. One of the walkways ended at a group of sculptures.

Near this complex of ball fields, he saw a river and across the river was what Joe called a "special train track." On the other side of the track was a raised highway that would lead to a multistory hospital, which he sketched as the camera crew recorded his effort. Once they found the hospital, they were to give the name of the missing person to the first nurse they encountered. Joe went on to describe the missing person as a man about seventy-seven years old.

When the crew went back to Japan, they started following the psychic clues. They quickly found out that there were thirteen Ferris wheels in Tokyo, but only four of them were covered with lights that changed colors. That immediately narrowed the focus to four locations. However, surprisingly, you could see ballparks with intersecting walkways from every one of those Ferris wheels. In all, at least sixteen ball fields were visible from atop the four big wheels.

Next, the crew began looking for sculptures at the end of a walkway, but they couldn't find any. They were ready to give up when they discovered a topiary garden—sculpted shrubbery—at the end of a path at the last location. That pathway also ended near the river that Joe had drawn. Across the river, they found a train track. It was a monorail, which was considered very special in Japan, just as Joe had described it.

They also found an elevated highway near the track, and after following it for twenty-eight miles, they came to a hospital. As they left their vehicle, they encountered a nurse walking across the parking lot and asked if she knew the man they were looking for. To the surprise of the crew, she said yes. She knew him because, just a few weeks ago, he'd been a patient. Did she know where he lived? Again, she surprised the crew. He lived just three blocks from the hospital, and she pointed out the house.

They went to the door and an elderly woman answered. They asked for the man by name, and she said she would get him. Everything checked out. They had found him! A short time later, the man, who was seventy-eight years old and had been missing for thirty-four years, was reunited with his son, who had instigated the search.

Thanks to the psychic abilities of Joe McMoneagle and the tenacious television crew that pursued his leads, the case was solved. In all, by the end of 2004, Joe had made ten trips to Tokyo for the television production company and found seven missing people.

I've known Joe McMoneagle since he read the manuscript of *PSI/NET*, a novel I co-authored with actor Billy Dee Williams. Since I've kept in touch with Joe, I knew what he was doing with the Japanese film crew in the above story. So the day before he appeared on Japanese television, I e-mailed my cousin, Russell Walstedt, a physicist who works in the nuclear power industry in Japan, and alerted him to the TV show. I knew he was skeptical about claims of psychic abilities so I was curious to hear his reaction.

So where does psychic power fit in the world of science? . . . Is it all just superstition or coincidence? The answer is a resounding no.

After watching it, he wrote back and said, "The remote viewing guy is indeed amazing, if actually genuine." He went on to point out that the crew was still looking for two of the three people they asked Joe to locate. However, Russell was baffled by how Joe had succeeded in locating even one of them.

Psychic Power in School

One day I asked a high school science teacher who lives in my neighborhood why parapsychology wasn't part of the curriculum. He seemed surprised by the question. "Well, we don't offer astronomy or entomology (the study of insects), either. There's no money for it and no one trained to teach it," he said. Then he added another reason, which indicated that money wasn't the only problem: "It's not really a science, you know, not like physics or biology."

"Why not?" I asked.

"Because psychic phenomena contradict the laws of nature, everything that science is based on."

Among scientists and educators, the topic of psychic powers is often met with skepticism and denial or dismissed as superstition and misguided thinking. Parapsychology isn't accepted by science because it's about unusual things that shouldn't happen. Yet they do!

Science and Psi

So where does psychic power fit in the world of science? Do the laws of science exclude such phenomenal abilities as those exhibited by Joe McMoneagle? Is it all just superstition or coincidence? The answer is a resounding no. In fact, psi has been the subject of extensive studies for more than one hundred years, and anyone who takes a close look at the results must admit that mental functioning can and does extend beyond the five senses.

However, don't be surprised if a scientist or science teacher informs you that psi doesn't stand up to scientific scrutiny. That's a commonly held viewpoint in the academic community. One of the reasons relates to the early scientific experiments in parapsychology, conducted from the 1880s to the beginning of the twentieth century. Researchers hailed the results as proof of psi, but later scrutiny revealed numerous instances of fraud. The researchers were duped and, as a result, critics said all the results were tainted.

But the view that there is no such thing as psychic phenomena is coming under increasing pressure to change. Over the decades, procedures for conducting experiments have improved immensely. Countless scientifically sound experiments in psychic phenomena have been conducted in laboratory conditions and repeated over and over again. The results point to the existence of psychic power.

Take this example carried out in 1933 by Dr. J. G. Pratt and his subject, Hubert Pearce. In the experiments conducted at Duke University, Pratt and Pearce were separated in different buildings that were more than one hundred yards apart. At an agreed time, Pratt began laying ESP cards face down. Known as Zener cards, they include a star, circle, square, cross, and wavy lines. The five cards are repeated five times in the deck. After going through the deck, Pratt turned the cards over and recorded them. The cards were shuffled and the procedure was repeated.

Meanwhile, in the other building, Pearce was writing down his guesses. To avoid any possibility of cheating, the cards were sealed in separate envelopes and given to another researcher,

Dr. J. B. Rhine, who compared the two lists. In all, Pearce made 1,859 guesses. Chance guesses would have resulted in 20 percent, or 370, correct guesses. The actual number of hits by Pearce was 558. The probability of those results occurring by chance is less than one in a hundred million.

The History of Psi Research

Dr. J. B. Rhine, considered the father of modern parapsychology, began research at Duke University in 1927 with Dr. Louisa E. Rhine, his colleague and wife. Rhine actually coined the terms *extrasensory perception* (ESP) to describe the apparent ability of some people to acquire information without the use of the known senses, and *parapsychology* to distinguish his interests from mainstream psychology. He also created the Zener deck, which is still used for experiments in telepathy, clairvoyance, and precognition.

By 1940, he and his associates had conducted thirty-three major studies involving almost a million trials. Twenty-seven of those experiments produced significant results. In 1966, Rhine's work was summarized in *Extra-Sensory Perception After Sixty Years*. In the five years following the publication of his results, different laboratories repeated his experiments thirty-three times. Twenty of them, or 61 percent, were statistically significant, meaning the results of those experiments supported the existence of ESP. Chance alone would have resulted in only 5 percent of the experiments duplicating Rhine's results. More about telepathy experiments, including those that followed Rhine's groundbreaking efforts, can be found in Chapter 3.

In spite of the successes of Rhine's work and that of other researchers, many scientists remain adamant that psi does not exist. The reasons are not always rational. As one scientist told parapsychologist Russell Targ, even if there were no fraud or irregularities in ESP experiments, he still wouldn't believe it.

Joe McMoneagle has found that some skeptics won't accept his results, even when he accurately identifies a target. That's what happened when he appeared on the National Geographic channel's *Naked Science* in an episode called *Telepathy*, broadcast February 16, 2005. He was given a photo of a young woman who was standing at a site somewhere in San Francisco. To determine the site, the producers had photographed six locations, put the photos in six envelopes, and numbered them one to six. Then, with the role of a die, one location was selected.

McMoneagle didn't see the photos or meet the woman who was going to the site. He was given half an hour to describe it. When he finished, Dr. Edward May, a scientist who like McMoneagle had no prior contact with the photos or the observer, studied the photos and picked out the ones that most closely matched McMoneagle's written description and drawings. His number one choice was the correct photo, the one that showed where the observer was standing.

McMoneagle had written that the woman had passed through a dark tunnel before reaching the site, then described a bridge that she was looking at and other details, including a circle and weird-looking art. She was, in fact, standing in a circle and looking at a bridge. To reach the parking lot she had passed through a dark underpass. The art consisted of two drawings and descriptive information that were on pedestals near the circle.

However, in spite of McMoneagle's apparent success in this double-blind experiment, his effort was given a thumbs down in the program's conclusion. The reasons: the correct selection of the photo "could have been a coincidence," and McMoneagle "didn't name the bridge." It was noted that there are other bridges in San Francisco.

Belief and the Sixth Sense

The power of belief apparently plays a significant role in the results of ESP experiments. One of the most important experiments in the history of psychic research was conducted by Dr. Gertrude Schmeidler in 1942. In what was known as the "sheep and goats" experiment, Schmeidler asked a group of her students to participate in telepathy tests using Zener cards. Before the experiment she asked which of them believed in psychic abilities and which thought it nonsense. She classified the believers as sheep and the skeptics as goats. The results showed that the sheep scored significantly above average in telepathy tests, while the goats scored below average. Left to chance, that result would be extremely unlikely; it meant that the goats somehow suppressed their psychic power to support their own intellectual convictions. In other words, their left brains sublimated their right brains' attempts at ESP. However, in doing so, their sixth sense left fingerprints all over the experiment. This result could well explain why many highly skeptical scientists, like the one Targ mentioned, have totally failed to obtain results in various tests for psi abilities.

Psychic power threatens the long-held beliefs of such scientists. They recognize that if science accepts that the mind has powers to gather information using means beyond our five senses, then many of the basic concepts of how reality works must change. So it's understandable that many of them are particularly slow to react and acknowledge the existence of psychic power, which will eventually change the course of science.

It should be noted, though, that some skeptical scientists have moved from disbelief to grudging acceptance that "something is going on." They recognize that the experiments are sound and the results show that psi exists. While they make that admission, they also say that it doesn't mean much, that the existence of psi won't change their worldview.

Such a contention follows the usual pattern for change in science. First, a new idea that doesn't fit the accepted pattern is rejected and ridiculed. Then, it is reluctantly accepted with the addendum that it's not significant. Finally, a new generation of scientists arrives and simply accepts the new idea as part of the current paradigm of science, and one-time skeptics say they knew it all along.

Scientists Who Used Their Psychic Power

It's fair to say that science is left-brain oriented. In other words, logic and reasoning are supreme. Right-brain thinking is about intuition, hunches, emotions, and imagination. It's the home base of all types of psi functioning, skills that are largely neglected by scientists, usually because they are considered too unreliable or too "soft." Yet, some prominent scientists have acknowledged that sources other than logic and rational thinking, including the murky waters of dreaming, have led them to great discoveries.

Friedrich Kekule, a nineteenth-century German chemist, was looking for the correct molecular structure of benzene when he found the answer in a dream. Atoms were dancing in his dream when they took the form of a snake biting its own tail. When he woke up, Kekule realized that the structure he was seeking was shaped like a circle.

After the physicist Niels Bohr dreamed that planets were attached to pieces of string that circled the sun, he was able to develop his theory about the movement of electrons. Likewise, Elias Howe invented the sewing machine after a dream in which he was attacked by natives brandishing spears with holes in the pointed ends. The dream image solved the problem of how to attach thread to the needle.

Albert Einstein recognized the validity and importance of the realm of right-brain thinking when he said, "The most beautiful and most profound emotion we can experience is the sensation of the mystical. It is the sower of all true science." While Einstein founded the new physics of quantum mechanics, it was a contemporary of Einstein named David Bohm who developed quantum theory in a way that allowed for the existence of psychic power. A key element of his work was the discovery of the nonlocal universe.

Where Is the Nonlocal Universe?

In the nonlocal universe, everything is interconnected in a vast web. Bohm called this web of connections, "quantum interconnectedness." That means that all of space-time is available to your consciousness. That includes other dimensions, the future, and the past! It's the realm of psychic power.

Bohm also talks about the *nonlocal mind*, which is our experience of the invisible interconnections—a hidden matrix—that hold the universe together. Essentially, the nonlocal mind and the nonlocal universe are one and the same. As physicist John Wheeler has said, "The stuff of the universe is mind stuff."

Although, in our everyday awareness, it may seem that everything is fragmented and unrelated rather than interconnected, quantum physicists say we are experiencing an illusion. It's as if we are looking at pieces of a puzzle without seeing the big picture. Our ability to find the doorway into the nonlocal universe is greatly limited by all the distractions around us and the constant internal chatter we hold with ourselves. Yet, it is possible to break through these barriers and connect to the vast matrix of the nonlocal universe. That's when your psychic power, the tool of the nonlocal mind, goes into action.

Here's another way to look at it. Think of phoning someone who lives in another part of the country. You need an area code, of course, before you can dial the number. Likewise, when you want to connect to the nonlocal universe you need to access a nonlocal code first. In this case, that code is psychic power.

In spite of the development of quantum physics, mainstream science remains as doubtful about the mysterious quantum world as it does about psychic phenomena. The old way of thinking about the universe still holds sway. In that view, each one of us is located in a particular point in space and time, and we are each separate from everyone and everything else.

However, in the last forty years, quantum physicists have said that model of the universe isn't correct. According to these modern physicists, consciousness is the building block of the universe, which is more like a great thought than a machine. Underlying our everyday world is another reality, where everything is interconnected. Furthermore, these physicists tell us that everything that exists originates in this realm—the nonlocal universe.

If new principles of physics, biology, or psychology do underlie psi experiences, then our current knowledge of human nature and the world around us is incomplete—and the world is a stranger and much richer place than science recognizes. Science often makes major advances in our understanding of the world through the consideration of anomalies—phenomena or data that do not fit into the thinking of the time. However, scientists are cautious about adopting radically new principles, and, as noted, they tend to be wary when faced with the evidence of experiments supporting psi phenomena. Typically, their response is to look for mistakes in the experiments so that the results can be discounted.

But when mainstream scientists accept the facts, the result ultimately could be revolutionary. Imagine psychic historians trained to explore the past through remote viewing. Similarly, doctors could use extrasensory perception to diagnose patients and psychokinesis to cure them. Physicists could directly explore subatomic particles, and astronomers could develop a new method of exploring other galaxies.

Got Psychic Power?

Don't confuse the exercises in *Psychic Power* with scientific experiments. Parapsychologists intentionally take away your control of the test. Their testing is a lot more rigid and controlled than the exercises you'll be doing here. You're not trying to prove that you've got psychic power to the world, only to yourself. Have fun while developing and testing your talents.

If you *are* successful, and you probably will be if you follow the exercises, don't be surprised if you encounter someone who doesn't believe it. The fact is, some people don't think anyone is psychic, and no matter how much proof you provide them it will never be enough. But, hey, that's their problem. Meanwhile, you can develop your skills and use them to better your life and help others.

Let's get right into it.

2 Becoming Aware

So how psychic are you? Maybe you remember one or more strange incidents in which you sensed something you shouldn't have known. Possibly it was a dream with a message that came true. An incredible synchronicity that defied all odds. Or a hunch that proved true. Maybe you felt wary about doing something but then were glad you listened to those feelings because nothing worked out as planned.

If you can remember such examples, jot them down in a notebook under a heading, such as "*My Psi Past.*" That way you'll have a record of whatever you remember. Leave space for additional incidents that you may recall later. The notebook will serve as a journal in your exploration of psychic power.

When you become more aware of these experiences and take note of them, you'll probably see that they happen more often than you realized. Or, they may start occurring more frequently just because you're investigating these matters.

For example, one day while working on this book, I woke up thinking about an acquaintance, whom I hadn't heard from in a couple of years. Later that morning, I got an e-mail from her and found out that she had recently given birth to a baby girl. However, if I hadn't been thinking about psychic abilities, I might have completely overlooked the incident. Now I've got a record of it, and you can do the same for your own experiences.

Test Your Psi Q

Maybe you *can't* recall any examples of psychic experiences. If that's the case, the following list of questions might help. It's a way of triggering your memory. As you read through the list, check the items that apply to you. Go over the ones you

checked and write down in your notebook any experiences that come to mind. You may realize that you are far more psychic than you thought.

Check the situations that apply to you. They are all examples of spontaneous psychic power.

- ✪ When I was young, I had an imaginary playmate.
- ✪ I've thought about a song, either the tune or the words, just moments before it came on the radio.
- ✪ I've said the exact same thing as a friend at the same time.
- ✪ I've read, thought, or spoken a word or phrase and simultaneously heard that word or phrase spoken on television or the radio.
- ✪ There have been times when I've known that the telephone was about to ring.
- ✪ I've thought about someone when, at that moment, the phone rang and it was that person.
- ✪ I've made decisions based on hunches and have been right.
- ✪ I've had a dream that contained a warning and it came true.
- ✪ I've glimpsed an incident that seemed like my imagination, and then it actually happened.
- ✪ I've gotten so involved in something at times that I was surprised by how much time went by.
- ✪ When I was young, I remember being confused about why other people didn't know things that seemed obvious to me.
- ✪ I've often guessed the right time to the exact minute.
- ✪ I've solved puzzling problems by getting a flash of inspiration as soon as I stop trying to solve them.
- ✪ At times, when first meeting someone, I've instantly

known that we would get along well.

✪ I've visited a place for the first time that felt familiar, as if I'd been there before.

✪ I've gotten confused about whether something happened to me in real life or in a dream.

Reasons for Wanting Psychic Power

By now you probably realize that you possess some psychic abilities. Next you may want to harness and expand your skills. Doing so requires imagination, a sense of curiosity and wonder, and a willingness to explore and succeed. However, before moving ahead, you should ask yourself an important question: Why exactly do you want to develop your psychic abilities? Check all the answers that apply to you. Jot down the choices you make in your notebook. I want to develop my psychic abilities so...

✪ *I can gain more control of my life.*
✪ *I can impress others with my powers.*
✪ *I can get others to do what I want.*
✪ *I can get whatever I want.*
✪ *I can get rich fast.*
✪ *I can solve all my problems.*
✪ *I can improve myself.*
✪ *I can help others.*
✪ *I can get answers to all my questions.*
✪ ....
(add your own answer).

It's natural that you might want to use your psychic abilities to improve your life. But what matters is how you use your abilities to achieve that goal. You're likely to be disappointed if you try to manipulate others with your talents.

Ultimately, psychic power is about becoming more rather than getting more.

Here are a few simple rules about psychic power that you might want to jot down in your notebook.

Psychic Power Guidelines

1) Be non-judgmental about your abilities. Step out of the way. Psychic power works best when you just let it happen.

2) Keep track of your progress.

3) Find time to relax and connect.

4) Be patient.

5) Never use psychic power to harm or endanger anyone.

6) Let your psychic power work for you. Integrate it into your daily life.

7) Help others whenever you can.

8) Be modest. Don't exaggerate your abilities.

Next, look at the following questions about major issues in your life. How many of them can you answer? Which ones do you really want to know? Write down the ones that really interest you. At the end of this chapter, we'll return to these questions and see how you can use your psychic power to find answers.

It's natural that you might want to use your psychic abilities to improve your life. But what matters is how you use your abilities to achieve that goal.

The Big Questions

✪ Who am I?
✪ What's my purpose in life?
✪ What do I want most?
✪ What do I fear most?
✪ What is my greatest talent?
✪ What will I be doing in five years or ten years?
✪ In what way am I my own worst enemy?

The Key to Psychic Power

I stumbled upon what I've come to believe is the key to developing psychic abilities when I was a teenager. But it took many years for me to put this knowledge to use. Here's the story of what I discovered and how I came upon it.

When I was growing up in a Minneapolis suburb, there was an old two-story wood frame house in the neighborhood on a large lot with many oak trees. The kids whispered about the place. Strange things happened in that house, we'd heard. The place was haunted and séances were held there late at night. The people who lived in the house were mysterious and exotic to us. They were from India and the women wore saris, the native garb of their land. The family was large, with many cousins, uncles, and aunts who came and went. Two of the brothers owned a small circus, and one summer the circus shut down for a couple of weeks in August and some of the animals were brought to the house. There were two elephants chained to stakes in the back yard, and at least one caged tiger and several monkeys.

Of course the animals attracted attention, and the notoriety of the house grew that summer. I mowed the family's lawn so I had some contact with them, which elevated my status in the neighborhood. I was a source of information and strange knowledge. A couple of my friends were interested in the rumors about séances and asked me to see if we could get invited to one. They figured the séances were probably held at midnight, or later, and we would have to sneak out.

I didn't think it was a good idea, especially since I was the one who had to do the talking. But they cajoled me, and finally I gave in. After the circus left and things calmed down, I mowed the lawn and collected the fifty cents I charged from the grand-mother in the household. As she paid me, I asked her if they really held séances.

She stared at me, frowned, and crossed her arms. Not a good sign. "No séances," she replied. I was about to make a hasty retreat when she added, "You want to talk to spirits? You can do it. But first you have to listen, and to do that you must quiet your mind."

My friends were disappointed that there were no séances, and they didn't understand what she meant. Was quieting your mind like holding your breath? We tried it and found that we could hold our breath a lot longer than we could stop thinking. Maybe she was just telling you to shut up, one of my friends said.

I wanted to ask her more questions, but I never had the chance. Summer was soon over, and that fall the family moved away. But I've always remembered the message from the old woman in the sari. *Quiet your mind*.

Since then I've learned that those three words are key not only to talking to spirits, but to developing all kinds of psychic abilities. In order to enter the realm of psychic power, you need to shift your awareness to create a direct link with your sub-conscious. So let's get right into it. I'll touch on some of the

*Quiet your mind.
. . . those
three words are
key not only to
talking to
spirits, but to
developing
all kinds of
psychic
abilities.*

basic concepts and then provide an exercise for relaxing your body and quieting your mind.

Making the Shift

Here's your chance to enter the state of mind where psychic power exists. Simply learning about psychic abilities, and not exploring them firsthand, is like reading about a thunderstorm versus getting caught in one, or studying a map of the Amazon as opposed to trekking along a trail in the vast rain forest.

In order to quiet your mind, you need to relax. When you enter a relaxed state, your brain waves slow until they slip into alpha, which is measured at eight to thirteen cycles per second. That compares to thirteen to thirty cycles per second in beta, your usual awakened state of mind. In alpha, you are relaxed but alert.

Finding Your Place

First, you need a quiet place to work where you won't be bothered. It could be your room or a corner of the basement or attic. You might even choose an outdoor location, if the weather is nice and the space is quiet.

You also need to pick the right time to practice. Maybe it's early in the morning right after you get up, in the evening before bed, or right after you get home from school. Try to stick with the same time and place.

Once you've decided on a location and time, you're ready to begin. You can either sit or lie down. You might try the floor with a cushion or two rather than a bed or couch. That way your body will know that when you go to the floor in one particular place at a particular time, you're headed toward relaxation. It's an especially good idea to avoid the bed where you normally sleep.

Eliminate all distractions—that means getting unplugged. Turn off the television, radio, cell phone, CD player, and computer. Loud music, radio or TV chatter, and ringing phones will block your access to psychic power. Send children and pets elsewhere. A dog licking you or a cat jumping on your lap can easily disrupt your efforts to move into a relaxed state of mind.

Turning Inward

Let's say you've arranged the perfect environment. You're home alone. All is peaceful. You've found a comfortable place to sit or lie down. You're ready to relax. It sounds easy. Anyone can do *that*. Hey, you can do it in your sleep. But the point is to do it while you're awake, and that's another matter.

Once you've eliminated all the potential external disruptions, you're ready to move into relaxation and deal with the internal disturbances, which can be even more troublesome. It's all about turning off the internal chatter, the continual conversation you have with yourself about what you did earlier, what you're going to do, and your reactions to everything that's going on around you. Don't expect immediate results. Even though quieting the mind means you're not really doing anything, it still may be one of the toughest things you'll ever attempt!

That's why I'm going to give you some exercises in focusing your mind, which will help you turn off that internal chatter. Take your time. Follow the exercises at your own pace. You can also listen to the CD, especially tracks one and two. Don't give up. With practice, you'll quickly enter that relaxed state where psychic power works.

Breathe!

As a yoga teacher, I've used many different techniques with my students for quieting the mind. The best way to begin is to

Even though quieting the mind means you're not really doing anything, it still may be one of the toughest things you'll ever attempt!

become aware of your breath. Normally we don't pay much attention to our breathing. It just happens on its own, an involuntary function, like the beat of your heart. But you can also control your breathing, just as you can tense and relax the muscles in your arm. As you read the following exercise, mentally work your way through your body, relaxing one part at a time.

At first, you'll probably spend several minutes entering a relaxed state. With practice, you'll be able to relax with a few deep breaths as you allow a wave of relaxation to gently flow through your body. Besides serving as the doorway to psychic power, relaxation also provides immediate stress relief, increased alertness, and enhanced creativity. Enjoy the process!

You can listen to track one on the CD for the following relaxation technique. Gradually, with practice, you may find that you enter a relaxed state easily so you can shorten the procedure. Eventually, you can dispense with the CD.

Exercise: Relax, Relax, Relax

Lie down and get comfortable. Become aware of your breathing. Focus on it. Take long, deep inhalations through your nose, pushing out your belly, and then exhaling through your nose as your belly sinks down. That's called diaphragmatic breathing. Your diaphragm contracts with the inhalation, making room for your lungs to expand, and it expands as you exhale.

Take several such breaths and, with each exhalation, let the tension start to drain out of your body. Let your eyelids get heavier with each breath and then allow your eyelids to close. Shift to gentle breathing.

Now, in order to enhance your relaxation, tense your body. It may seem contradictory to tense muscles in order to relax, but you'll see how the process works. Make tight fists with your hands. Tense your shoulders, then lift your arms a couple of inches.

Next, curl your toes and tense your feet, thighs, and buttocks. Lift your legs a couple of inches. Arch your back, bringing your shoulder blades closer together, and tense your chest. Now hold your breath and squeeze all the muscles in your face toward your nose. Tense the entire body for several seconds, then release and relax. Notice the difference between your tensed and your relaxed body.

Now imagine invisible fingers massaging your scalp, your forehead, temples, then around your eye sockets, over the bridge of your nose, along your cheeks, and down your jaw. Leave a slight gap between your teeth and let the tongue come down from the roof of your mouth.

Relax all the muscles in your neck, and follow the muscles in the back of your neck over your shoulders. Relax your upper arms, elbows, forearms, wrists, hands, and fingers. Relax, relax, relax.

Now imagine a wave of relaxation rolling down over your chest and back and sides. Let the lower back and belly relax. Let the hipbones relax in the hip sockets. The buttocks relax, the backs of the thighs relax, the tops of the thighs relax.

Kneecaps float on the knees, and the backs of the knees relax. Shins and the muscles in the calves relax. Ankles, feet, and toes relax. Feel the bottoms of your feet relax. Internal organs relax, mind relax.

You'll no doubt find that your mind soon starts to wander. You can gently release your thoughts and return to focusing on your breathing. You might imagine your breath as a stream of white light coming into the lungs and out again. Let your breath guide you into an even deeper state of relaxation.

Creating images with your mind as you relax is called visualization. Here's another image you can visualize to help you stay focused.

Exercise: Entering the Garden

Once you're relaxed, imagine a beautiful place in nature. It might be a meadow surrounded by mountains, a tranquil lake or pond, or a waterfall surrounded by a forest. Find your "garden," a place that you can come back to over and over again. See yourself inside the garden. Maybe you are seated comfortably on the ground or on a smooth rock.

Notice how you feel. You should be relaxed, but alert. Pay attention to the details of your surroundings, the rich smells of the earth and forest, the sounds of nature, the colors and shapes. You are in the realm of psychic power now. Watch for anything unusual. You might hear a voice or even see a person or animal, a messenger who arrives with some advice.

As you wait, don't be surprised or frustrated if your mind tends to wander. Try stepping outside your thoughts. First, you become aware that you are thinking. Maybe you're evaluating what you're doing. *Why am I doing this? How long is it going to take? This is boring. Is this really worth my time?* You might start thinking about your plans. *Maybe we'll go to a movie tonight.* Or your thoughts might turn to your physical concerns. *I'm getting hungry.*

Imagine that the real you is not the one thinking, but the one observing the thinker. See if you can become the observer. Tell yourself, *Think all you want. I'll be over here in the garden watching.* And that's when something might happen…a voice in your head that's not your conscious thought…a brief image or a vision. Remember it, record it.

Next you'll get a chance to move deeper into your psychic power. Go back to the questions on page 20 and pick out one that interests you. Or, you can create your own question. But make it something important. If you come up with a trivial question, you can expect a trivial answer, if any. Keep your question in mind as you begin.

Exercise: Your Own Private Theater

Either lying down or seated in your special place, close your eyes and take several deep breaths, relaxing your body with each exhalation. Then imagine that you're entering a building and walking over to an elevator. The door opens, you step inside. Rather than the first floor, you're on the tenth floor. You see the number above the door. You press the button for the first floor and the door closes. You feel the elevator slowly descending and you see the number 9. After a few seconds, you see 8, then 7…6…5…all the way down.

With each floor you feel yourself becoming more relaxed. When you reach the first floor, the door opens and you step out onto thick carpeting in a hallway. You walk to the double doors at the end of the hall and step into a dimly lit private theater. There's a large screen on the wall and a comfortable chair. It's your chair and you settle into it. You look toward the screen and suddenly it's right in front of you. It's almost as if the screen surrounds you and you're inside it.

You see the color red on the screen. The red shifts to orange, and you feel even more relaxed. Orange turns to yellow...then green...blue... purple...and violet. As each color appears, you take a deep breath and exhale. You feel yourself going deeper into relaxation.

The screen goes dark. For a moment, think about the question you picked as you started. Let it go and watch what unfolds. On your first attempt, you may not get any viable results. But as you visualize the elevator and the theater, you'll find out whether psychic power works best for you through vision, hearing, or feelings.

Gradually, an image may appear or a scene may unfold. You may feel as if you're inside the scene. Or you might only hear a voice. You might just get a sense of intuitive knowing. Whatever happens, you might find an answer to your question. Even if you think the answer doesn't relate to your question, don't judge it or dismiss it. The image may be symbolic. You can figure out its meaning later.

As you finish your session, release the image of the theater. Write down in your journal whatever you saw, heard, or felt. However your question is answered, whether you understand it or not, know that you are on your way.

A modified version of this exercise is found on track two of the CD.

★ ★ ★

Experiments
have shown
hat telepathy,
or mind-to-
mind commu-
ication, works
est when the
eople involved
have close
ties.

★ ★ ★

You've probably heard someone say, "Hey, I was just thinking the same thing" or "I was just about to call you." Chances are that person was someone you know well. Experiments have shown that telepathy, or mind-to-mind communication, works best when the people involved have close ties.

Imagine you've just visited your elderly mother who lives alone. You're almost home when you hear her voice in your head calling to you. You try to ignore it. You're going to be late for a meeting if you don't hurry. But the voice continues calling your name, and you know it's your mother. So you call her on your cell phone, but there's no answer. That's odd. She wasn't going anywhere. You turn around and head back to her apartment. You find her on the floor, unable to get up and reach the phone to call for help. You're concerned about her, but you're also relieved that you came back.

Telepathy

Of all the types of psychic effects, telepathy has received the most interest and scrutiny. Throughout history, sending and receiving information by means of a sixth sense has been a professed ability for certain talented individuals and a spontaneous experience for many others. In some so-called primitive cultures, telepathy was known as one of the many psychic abi'ities of the shamans or healers.

Anthropologists studying such cultures have observed bers communicating over long distances through telepᴀ means. High in the Andes, the Q'ero people, descen⸍ Incas, use telepathy like we use telephones, accor ical anthropologist Alberto Villoldo, who has st for more than two decades. Studies of the aʰ

3 Mind-to-Mind

watching. And that's when something might happen…a voice in your head that's not your conscious thought…a brief image or a vision. Remember it, record it.

Next you'll get a chance to move deeper into your psychic power. Go back to the questions on page 20 and pick out one that interests you. Or, you can create your own question. But make it something important. If you come up with a trivial question, you can expect a trivial answer, if any. Keep your question in mind as you begin.

Exercise: Your Own Private Theater

Either lying down or seated in your special place, close your eyes and take several deep breaths, relaxing your body with each exhalation. Then imagine that you're entering a building and walking over to an elevator. The door opens, you step inside. Rather than the first floor, you're on the tenth floor. You see the number above the door. You press the button for the first floor and the door closes. You feel the elevator slowly descending and you see the number 9. After a few seconds, you see 8, then 7…6…5…all the way down.

With each floor you feel yourself becoming more relaxed. When you reach the first floor, the door opens and you step out onto thick carpeting in a hallway. You walk to the double doors at the end of the hall and step into a dimly lit private theater. There's a large screen on the wall and a comfortable chair. It's your chair and you settle into it. You look toward the screen and suddenly it's right in front of you. It's almost as if the screen surrounds you and you're inside it.

You see the color red on the screen. The red shifts to orange, and you feel even more relaxed. Orange turns to yellow…then green…blue… purple…and violet. As each color appears, you take a deep breath and exhale. You feel yourself going deeper into relaxation.

The screen goes dark. For a moment, think about the question you picked as you started. Let it go and watch what unfolds. On your first attempt, you may not get any viable results. But as you visualize the elevator and the theater, you'll find out whether psychic power works best for you through vision, hearing, or feelings.

Gradually, an image may appear or a scene may unfold. You may feel as if you're inside the scene. Or you might only hear a voice. You might just get a sense of intuitive knowing. Whatever happens, you might find an answer to your question. Even if you think the answer doesn't relate to your question, don't judge it or dismiss it. The image may be symbolic. You can figure out its meaning later.

As you finish your session, release the image of the theater. Write down in your journal whatever you saw, heard, or felt. However your question is answered, whether you understand it or not, know that you are on your way.

A modified version of this exercise is found on track two of the CD.

You've probably heard someone say, "Hey, I was just thinking the same thing" or "I was just about to call you." Chances are that person was someone you know well. Experiments have shown that telepathy, or mind-to-mind communication, works best when the people involved have close ties.

Imagine you've just visited your elderly mother who lives alone. You're almost home when you hear her voice in your head calling to you. You try to ignore it. You're going to be late for a meeting if you don't hurry. But the voice continues calling your name, and you know it's your mother. So you call her on your cell phone, but there's no answer. That's odd. She wasn't going anywhere. You turn around and head back to her apartment. You find her on the floor, unable to get up and reach the phone to call for help. You're concerned about her, but you're also relieved that you came back.

Telepathy

Of all the types of psychic effects, telepathy has received the most interest and scrutiny. Throughout history, sending and receiving information by means of a sixth sense has been a professed ability for certain talented individuals and a spontaneous experience for many others. In some so-called primitive cultures, telepathy was known as one of the many psychic abilities of the shamans or healers.

Anthropologists studying such cultures have observed members communicating over long distances through telepathic means. High in the Andes, the Q'ero people, descendants of the Incas, use telepathy like we use telephones, according to medical anthropologist Alberto Villoldo, who has studied the Q'eros for more than two decades. Studies of the aborigines in

3 Mind-to-Mind

Australia found that villagers knew when a hunting party was returning, even though the hunters often traveled for several days.

But telepathy isn't disappearing with the demise of traditional cultures and the advance of technological wonders. Biologist Rupert Sheldrake believes we may be using telepathy without even realizing it. He notes that many people have experienced "telephone telepathy." "The evolution of telepathy is still going on," Sheldrake notes. "After telephone telepathy comes e-mail telepathy, which generally follows the same patterns. You think of someone you haven't contacted for a while, and shortly afterwards receive an e-mail from that person."

On numerous occasions, I've decided to e-mail a friend or associate and before I can do it, I receive an e-mail from that individual, sometimes addressing the very question on my mind. I've also received e-mail responses from people who said they were just about to write to me when my e-mail arrived.

While such examples of spontaneous telepathy could be dismissed as coincidental, telepathy is often far more explicit when it involves intense emotions, such as distress or fear. In such cases, you might hear the person's voice, or see an image of the sender—usually someone close to you—or experience a strong feeling or impression. The need to communicate, as in the following example from author Bernard Gittelson, can overcome distance and other barriers that prevent contact in the usual ways.

Joicey Acker Hurth of Cedarburg, Wisconsin, described a telepathic distress call she received from her 5-year-old daughter, Joicey. She was standing in front of her sink when, she recalled, "Suddenly I froze and dropped the plate I was holding. I raised my eyes to heaven and said, 'Oh God, don't let her get killed.'" She immediately phoned the nearby theater where

Joicey had gone to meet her father and brother. When a girl answered, Mrs. Hurth blurted that her daughter had an accident and she wanted to know if she was badly hurt. The girl was baffled and said that the accident just happened—how did she know? Mrs. Hurth found out that her daughter had been hit by a car, but she wasn't badly hurt. Joicey's father was taking her to the hospital. Later, Mrs. Hurth learned that her daughter had sat on the curb after the accident and called out, "Mama, Mama, Mama."

Sometimes individuals who are particularly perceptive pick up subtle distress calls. Millie Germondo of Lumberport, West Virginia, recalls getting an impression of a friend, Evelyn, telling her that she was dying. She worried about her friend and finally called her. Millie was relieved to hear her voice and explained the impression she'd received. Evelyn laughed and said, "I'm alive, but I've got the flu and earlier I was feeling like I *was* going to die."

Family Connections

Family members sometimes experience telepathic connections when no distressful emotions are involved. One family member, for example, might inadvertently sense what the other one is thinking and say it. Or, he or she may finish the other person's sentence.

Skeptics would respond that, in such instances, you are simply picking up subtle sensory cues. In other words, you know the person well and can guess what she's thinking or about to say by the way she looks or acts, or by what you've been talking about. Alternately, they might also say that it was just coincidental.

Dr. Berthold Schwarz, a South Florida psychiatrist and paranormal researcher, says such telepathic communications could be a combination of sensory cues *and* intuitive knowing. Schwarz carried out a detailed study of parent-child telepathy when his children were growing up in New Jersey. He and his wife recorded incidents of telepathy they experienced with their two children, Eric and Lisa. He published his findings in *Parent-Child Telepathy: A Study of the Telepathy of Everyday Life*, which included more than five hundred incidents that took place during a nine-year period. What's particularly interesting is that Schwarz's research didn't focus on crises but on trivial incidents from everyday life.

For example, Schwarz describes the following episode:

"I was comfortably seated in an easy chair looking at a topographic map, with Lisa standing beside me. I noted on the map for the first time Stickle Pond...It was quite intriguing. I thought, 'Hmm, a nature lake, must be beautiful.' Hardly had these fleeting thoughts occurred to me when Lisa burst out, 'Stickle Pond, is that a natural pond or not?' There are at least 75 ponds, of which more than 35 appear on the U.S. Government topographical map. Lisa, who was behind me, could not see my eyes."

In another incident, Schwarz was walking with Lisa in their backyard after dinner. He writes: "While going down the hill and holding on to her hand, I noticed a few stray leaves on the ground from the pear and apple trees. The thought crossed my mind, 'I wonder if the pear tree will die with these leaves coming down?' Lisa then verbally repeated the same words. When I asked her why she thought that, she said, 'Mommy said so.' I later checked with Ardis, who said she has never commented on the pear tree or any other trees to Lisa. During the walk Lisa was very affectionate."

Most people might see Schwarz's research as a seemingly harmless exploration of the mind's potential. Yet when I met Schwarz in the mid-1980s after he moved to Florida, he was under attack by a debunker who sent two magicians to trick him into believing they had psychic abilities in an attempt to belittle his previous work. (Debunkers are profound disbelievers who dogmatically maintain there is no sixth sense and that all psychic abilities, regardless of the massive evidence to the contrary, are misinterpretations of normal phenomena or clever tricks.) In spite of the efforts to undermine him, Schwarz continued his paranormal research for many years, even exploring UFO-related abduction cases, a subject that most scientists ignored at all costs.

Group Telepathy

Although telepathy typically involves extrasensory communication between two people, groups of people also can experience mind-to-mind communication. Psychic researcher Russell Targ provides an example of such communication that took place during a meeting hosted by Dr. Dean Brown. At one point, Brown said he was interested in how people can instantly know whether they've ever heard a word or name. For example, he asked Targ and the other four people who had joined him what the word *churk* means.

Immediately, Targ and the others raised their hands. Brown looked baffled and exclaimed, "How could you know what it means? I just made up the word!"

However, just before attending the meeting, the group of five had eaten at a Cuban restaurant that offered a catfish special with churk sauce. Targ said the only plausible answer was that Brown had accessed the word from their minds. That conclusion was further supported when Targ went back to the restaurant and found out that the sauce is actually called *jerk*, but the waitress, who was from El Salvador, had difficulty pronouncing the "j" sound. So the five at the table had heard the word as churk.

Targ called the experience an example of "almost pure telepathy." The only other possible explanation, he said, would be *retrocognitive clairaudience*—that is, the experience of psychically hearing something that occurred in the past.

Projecting Psychic Power

While many dramatic instances of telepathy occur spontaneously, telepathy can also occur intentionally, as laboratory tests have shown. Some of the first scientific experiments were conducted in the mid-nineteenth century and involved subjects who were hypnotized. In one experiment, a Scottish surgeon, James Esdaile, hypnotized and blindfolded a man who he knew was a viable subject because the man had undergone surgery using hypnosis as anesthesia. In this instance, Esdaile tried to telepathically send tastes and smells to the man, the receiver. With an assistant as an intermediary, Esdaile sampled substances such as salt, brandy, and a lime. When the assistant gave Esdaile a partially rotten lime to taste, the subject made a wry face and said, "I taste a nasty old lime." He was equally successful with the other substances.

In the 1880s, the Society of Psychical Research set out to see if telepathy was possible *without* hypnosis. The term *telepathy* actually didn't come into use until 1882 when it was coined by F. W. H. Myers, one of the founders of the society. They soon found that sensitive individuals could detect distant tastes and smells, and also pain, such as a pinch or a pinprick, while remaining in their normal state of consciousness.

Other Victorian-era experiments in telepathy involved games in which objects were hidden. Then came experiments with cards in which the receiver would attempt to guess the suit of playing cards. There was a 25 percent chance of guessing a card correctly, so a higher percentage, after a large number of trials, would indicate the existence of telepathy. By 1886, more than 17,000 trials had been carried out with an average success rate of 26.5 percent. Although that doesn't sound very impressive, the result with that many trials involved was significantly above the chance level according to statistical tests.

Decades later, the era of modern parapsychology would begin with the now famous experiments conducted by J. B. Rhine and his wife. Those experiments using Rhine's Zener cards are described in Chapter 1.

Another type of experiment involved the sending and receiving of pictures. One person focused on the picture while the other person attempted to draw it. In *Mental Radio* (1930), Upton Sinclair described a successful series of such experiments that he conducted with his wife. She would lie in semi-darkness and sketch images that were surprisingly similar to what Sinclair or other family members sent.

If you're anxious to try your own experiments in receiving telepathic images, start with a few simple methods. Here's one you can do right away without a partner being actively involved.

Exercise: Guessing Who's There

When the telephone rings, guess who it is before you answer. (If you're expecting a call, that doesn't count. In such a case, you're using logic rather than psychic power.) Don't get frustrated if you guess the wrong person. Keep practicing and you'll see your skills improving. Sometimes you'll think of the person moments before the phone rings. Alternately, when you happen to think of someone and the phone fails to ring, you might call and find out if the person was thinking of you.

Exercise: Receiving Images

Here's a fun exercise to try with a friend. Tell your friend to mentally select a fruit. She should see the fruit clearly: the color and shape, the texture, even the taste. The friend should repeat the name of the fruit silently as she sends an image to you.

Clear your mind. Write down the impressions you receive. Can you taste the fruit? What color is it? How does it feel? Don't spend more than one minute on the target. Try other targets, such as vegetables or flowers.

Exercise: Picking Zener Cards

You can make your own Zener card deck for this exercise. Use three-by-five-inch index cards. Draw the symbols: a star, three parallel wavy lines, a cross or plus sign, a circle, and a square. Make five sets of each for a total of twenty-five cards. When the cards are ready, take a few minutes to prepare yourself by moving into a relaxed state. Don't forget to take several deep breaths.

When you're ready, the sender should focus on the first card, then project the image to you. Write down the image that comes to mind. Go through the deck that way. The sender should take care to keep the cards in order. After the last card, compare your list with the deck by turning the deck right side up so that the first card is now on top.

Odds are that by chance you will correctly identify five cards. If your score is higher than five, that indicates possible psychic functioning. Of course, you'll need to go through the deck a few more times before you can get a clearer picture. But don't overdo it. After going through the deck three times, the

process may become tedious or your accuracy may drop. So take a break. You can try more later.

Exercise: Telepathic Sketches

If you're testing your ability to receive images, have your partner cut out ten photographs from a magazine. Each one should be unique. Don't use head shots of people. Scenic landscapes, buildings, or action photos are preferable as long as they're distinct. Make sure that you don't see them in advance. When you're relaxed and the sender is ready, he should retreat to a separate room, randomly select one of the photos, and send it to you telepathically.

Write down or sketch your impressions, even if they are fleeting. After a couple of minutes, your partner should move to another photo. Make sure the photos and your responses are numbered. Afterwards, compare your drawings or comments to the photos.

Alternately, your friend can make simple drawings instead of using photos. But avoid geometric shapes in favor of illustrations that represent tangible objects. As you concentrate on receiving an image, try to avoid analyzing the impressions you are getting. In other words, if you draw lines that resemble a spiderweb, don't draw a spider. Stay with the intuitive sense of the image. What looks like a spiderweb might be the branches of a tree.

Dream Telepathy

If you're having trouble picking up images from a sender, try to do it in your sleep. Researchers say that receiving telepathic messages is easier in the dream state than while you're awake. Your sender can project the image of a photo to you after you're asleep. When you wake up, jot down any dreams you remember. Probably the best time to send an image is within an hour of your regular wake-up time. Dreams during that period are the ones that are most easily remembered.

Experiments in dream telepathy were conducted in the 1960s by psychiatrist Montague Ullman and psychologist Stanley Krippner at the Maimonides Medical Center in Brooklyn. Electrodes were attached to the head of a volunteer who slept at the laboratory. When monitors showed that the sleeper had entered the rapid eye movement (REM) phase of sleep, known for dream activity, a sender would focus on a picture and attempt to transmit the image to the sleeping receiver. The picture was chosen at random from eight possibilities. A short while later, the subject would be awakened and asked to recount her dream. Later, independent judges compared the dream description with the eight photos and selected the photo that was closest to the dream images.

In one case, the receiver reported dreaming about "an Oriental man, a fountain, water spray, walking down the street when it was raining." The target photograph was a painting: Hiroshige's *Downpour at Shono*. In another case, the subject dreamed about going to Madison Square Garden and buying tickets for a boxing match. The target was a painting of a boxing match.

Altogether, 450 dream telepathy sessions were reported between 1966 and 1973. The result was 63 percent accuracy with a chance level of 50 percent. The odds of hitting 63 percent were one in 75 million chances, which definitely suggested that dream telepathy was real.

Ganzfeld Telepathy Experiments

As the dream telepathy experiments were ending in the early 1970s, a new form of telepathy experiments began. Known as *ganzfeld*, a German word that means "whole field," these experiments emphasized the use of white noise, such as the static between radio stations, as a means of reducing sensory stimulation and creating a state of mind conducive to psychic functioning. So, instead of sleeping, the subject enters a relaxed, meditative state of mind.

In the experiments, a subject sits in a comfortable chair listening to white noise through headphones. Ping-pong balls cut in half cover the person's eyes. Often, a ten-minute relaxation tape is played at the outset. When the receiver is ready, the scientist in charge of the experiment selects the target picture from one of four sealed envelopes. He then hands the sealed envelope to the sender, who is in a separate room. The sender opens the envelope, focuses on the picture, and tries to project the image to the receiver. The sender alternately projects and relaxes over a twenty-minute period.

After the session ends, the four images are shown to the receiver, who then ranks the images in order from the most likely target to the least likely. If the projected image is number one, it's considered a hit. If not, it's a miss. On the basis of chance, the receiver should select the correct image 25 percent of the time. A higher percentage over repeated trials suggests that telepathy is at work. The experiments, conducted over more than twenty-five years by many labs in several countries, have provided impressive results and indicate that telepathy is possible under laboratory conditions.

During the time that the images are being sent, the receiver is encouraged to talk into a recorder and explain the images that are coming to mind. Here are comments from recordings of two subjects who spoke during experiments conducted by para-psychologist Charles Honorton.

The target: Salvador Dalí's famous painting of Christ crucified.

The receiver's comments: I think of guides, like spirit guides, leading me and I come into like a court with a king. It's quite…it's like heaven. The king something like Jesus. Woman. Now I'm just sort of somersaulting through heaven…brooding… Aztecs, the Sun God…high priest…fear….graves. Woman. Prayer…funeral…dark. Death…souls…Ten Commandments. Moses….

The target: A video clip of five horses galloping in a snow-storm from the film *The Lathe of Heaven.* The scene shifts to a single horse trotting in a grassy meadow, first at normal speed, then in slow motion. Then the same horse is trotting slowly through city streets.

The receiver's comments: I keep going to the mountains….It's snowing…. Moving again, this time to the left, spinning to the left…spinning. Like on a carousel, horses. Horses on a carousel, a circus….

Exercise: Telepathic Call Return

Here's an exercise that focuses on reaching others, who are unaware of your efforts, through telepathic projection. Pick someone you want to call you. Begin with someone who is like-ly to call you, a person who might easily decide to give you a call. Write down the target's name. Now relax. Breathe deeply. Imagine a scene where the person might be. If you know exact-ly where the person is and what the surroundings look like, then visualize it.

Next, focus on the person. Picture his face and what he might be doing. Now imagine him smiling as he decides to give you a call. Imagine him dialing your number on his phone. You answer and he identifies himself and asks how you are. Focus for a few minutes, then let go of the image. Think about something else.

If you don't get a call in the next several minutes, call him. Ask him what he's doing and if he'd been thinking about you. He might've thought about calling you but got too busy. If so, ask about what time he was thinking of calling you. See if it corresponds with when you were sending him a message.

If the answer is no, then try another person.

Exercise: Telepathic Emotions

With any telepathic projection, you want to avoid making another person uneasy or doing anything to cause harm. With this exercise, you can brighten someone's day by sending an emotion that she needs to help balance her feelings. It might be kindness, compassion, love, optimism, encouragement, hope, or something else that's appropriate. Picture your subject and, after relaxing, imagine a silver cord connecting the two of you. Next see a ripple of energy moving along the cord from you to the subject. Know that what you send will be helpful, creating harmony and causing no harm.

Note the time of the projection and check with the person later to see if she noticed any shift in energy or experienced the emotion that you were sending. Keep in mind that while you can send an emotion, you can't force anyone to receive it, no matter how beneficial it might be. Keep practicing this one and watch for positive results.

Pet Telepathy

If you have a dog or cat, you might've noticed that your pet sometimes seems to respond telepathically to your thoughts. People who train animals typically are well aware of this factor. Barbara Woodhouse, a British dog trainer and author of *How Your Dog Thinks*, says: "You should always bear in mind that the dog picks up your thoughts by an acute telepathic sense, and it is useless to be thinking one thing and saying another; you cannot fool a dog."

In *The Sense of Being Stared At*, Rupert Sheldrake cites the story of Teresa McKenzie of Carmel Valley, California, who suspected her dog picked up her thoughts. One day, while taking a bath, she tested her suspicion. Her dog was sleeping in another room. She pictured herself far away from her dog and silently called to the dog to come to her. "To my astonishment, I heard her get up in the living room, and shake off her sleepiness," Teresa said. "She walked into the bathroom, came up next to the tub, yawned and stretched, and looked at me as if to say, 'You rang?'"

At the time I read that story my golden retriever, Jessie, was sleeping in another room. She'd gotten up early with my daughter who leaves for school at 6:30 A.M., then after a couple of hours went back to sleep. I saw myself calling to her from a distance. I repeated her name to myself several times. A couple of minutes passed and I figured she was deep in sleep and not willing to respond, if she even heard me. Then, to my surprise, I heard her nails clicking across the tile floor as she left the living room and walked to my study. She stopped at my doorway and looked puzzled as if to say, "So what do you want?"

Telepathy between humans and animals can work both ways. A few years ago, our cat named Fox disappeared. The female cat rarely strayed far from home so we knew something had happened to her. I quieted my mind and focused on Fox, calling mentally to her over and over to come home. I felt that she heard me, that she wanted to come home, but couldn't do so. Several days had already passed, but I was convinced that she would return home within three days. I told Trish, "Fox will be home by Saturday."

Saturday night, just before midnight, we heard a knock on our kitchen door. We opened it to find our next-door neighbor, a fellow cat owner, holding Fox. She had just come home, heard a cat meowing, and found Fox in the courtyard we shared. Fox's front paws were rubbed raw as if she'd been scratching to get out of a container, possibly a cat carrier. She'd been held by someone against her will and had finally escaped. She'd even made it by my deadline.

Susan Chernak McElroy, author of *Animals as Teachers & Healers*, cites a peculiar tale of a telepathic puffer fish that swam up to a vacationing dentist as he snorkeled the waters off Hawaii. He thought the fish was struggling as if it were sick, and he silently asked it to come closer if it wanted help. When the fish did so, he noticed a hook in its mouth with line attached and connected to a heavy lead sinker. He slowly dragged the fish to the beach after explaining what he needed to do. When he reached shore, he wrapped the line around a rock, retrieved pliers, and removed the hook. He released the fish, which swam away, its life saved.

A couple of days later, while snorkeling with a friend in the same area, he wondered if the puffer fish was still around. He called out in his mind to the fish, and to his surprise a pair of puffer fish, typically shy creatures, swam toward him and his friend. He mentally asked, "Are you my friend?" One of the fish turned vertical, revealing a mouth recently injured by a hook. The two fish swam near the snorkelers for half an hour.

Exercise: Calling Your Pet

1) As with the previous examples, try mentally calling your dog or cat from another room. Make sure you send an image as well as calling your pet's name. See yourself separated by a distance from your dog and calling out.

2) Alternately, you can send an image of food or a treat. Picture in your mind that you're feeding your dog or cat its favorite food or offering a treat. See your pet walking up to you as you set down the food. Add as much detail as you want. See the cat arching its back as you stroke it. Listen to it purr in contentment as it begins to eat. Or, see your dog gobbling down its chow or begging for a treat. Repeat the images again. See if your pet has responded either by coming to you or moving to the feeding area.

3) You can also try calling your pets while you're on your way home. In this exercise, you'll need to work with a partner. Alert your partner of your plans and the approximate time of your arrival home. Make sure you call far enough in advance so that the animal's response isn't triggered by the call. When you're within a few minutes of home, send out an image to your pet showing your arrival. See yourself happily greeting the animal. Mentally call out its name several times and resend the image of the reunion a couple more times. When you arrive, your pet will probably be waiting for you. Find out from your partner when the animal went to the door or window to look for you. If it was before your pet could see or hear your vehicle, then you were successful.

The Bigger Picture

Telepathy might be one of the easiest elements of psychic power to obtain. Three out of four people say they have experienced telepathic communication. Being adept at receiving telepathic messages gives you an edge. Besides being able to detect telepathic calls for help in emergency situations, you can use the skills in your daily life. With practice, you can pick up information about people that may not be otherwise readily apparent.

Imagine that you're buying a house and everything seems perfect. It's everything you're looking for: the right size, the right neighborhood, the right price. However, there's something the seller isn't telling you. You're sure of it. You feel a nudge, a voice tells you to keep asking questions to find out what's wrong. You look around outside again and go to the backyard. You ask about the vacant lot behind the house, and finally it comes out. That property has been zoned for commercial use, and a car wash will be built right behind the house. You're glad you asked.

But what about telepathic projection? What are the advantages of being able to send messages? How can it help you in your daily life? Why not just pick up the phone or send an e-mail? Why bother concentrating so hard?

The answer is that you are already projecting more than you realize. Your life conditions—where you live and how you live, what you do and how you do it, who you associate with and how you associate with them—are essentially a reflection of what you project on a daily basis. Improving your projection skills with telepathic experiments will show you the power you possess and help you become more aware of what you already are projecting to the world. Through practice, you can clarify your goals and improve your life.

4 Getting in Sync

Y ou've probably heard it said that someone happened to be in the right place at the right time. It was just a coincidence. Pure luck. That's all. That's how he got where he is. Maybe you've said such things yourself.

But let's take a little closer look here at what we call luck or coincidence. Maybe there's something more to it: something called synchronicity or meaningful coincidence.

For example, as I began gathering information for this chapter I picked up a book called *Intuition: The Path to Inner Wisdom* by Patricia Einstein. There was no mention of synchronicity in the table of contents and no index. So I casually opened the book and my gaze immediately fell onto a chapter subheading called "Getting in Sync." Below that, I read the following:

"We've all had the experience of being in the right place at the right time, and at some point in our lives we've all known someone whom we characterized as lucky. Luck, however, is not a matter of chance. It's really a question of synchronicity."

How appropriate. I'd found a perfect quote to begin the chapter. Even though I didn't know if the word *synchronicity* would be found in the book, I was, you could say, at the right place at the right time. It was just what I needed.

Such experiences are probably the most common type of spontaneous psychic experiences, but we often dismiss them as luck or chance. As Bernard Gittelson put it in *Intangible Evidence:* "Many of us…lead our lives convinced that coincidence runs rampant, but if we computed the frequency of such coincidences and compared them to statistical possibilities, our argument for coincidence simply wouldn't stand up."

In other words, something greater than randomness is at work. Synchronicity offers us a peek at a grander picture of reality, one that's normally hidden from our view. It's the process of aligning with a larger awareness.

Coincidence vs. Synchronicity

So is every coincidence a synchronicity? The difference between the two lies in the term *meaningful*. Synchronicity is a coincidence with meaning or relevance. For example, a couple of days after I found the previous quote, another similar experience occurred. I'd just come into my home office after looking at Venus through a telescope while the planet was in close proximity to the crescent moon.

I returned to my research on synchronicity and opened Gittelson's book. Immediately, the word *Venus* popped out at me. So I read a comment about an author pondering why we can't see Venus during the day. The book was 615 pages and had nothing to do with Venus or astronomy. There was no logical connection between my viewing of Venus and reading a comment about the planet moments later. Yet it happened. On one level it was a coincidence. However, the fact that I was writing and researching synchronicity made it meaningful for me. In other words, I was looking for information on synchronicity, and I experienced one.

Forever Jung

You can't talk about synchronicity very long without mentioning Carl Jung. After all, the Swiss psychiatrist coined the term. In describing meaningful coincidences, or events related by their significance rather than by their causes, he wrote:

"This ... involves a certain curious principle that I have termed 'synchronicity', a concept that formulates a point of view diametrically opposed to that of causality. Since the latter is merely statistical truth and not absolute, it is a sort of working hypothesis of how events evolve one out of another, whereas synchronicity takes the coincidence of events in space and

★★★

So is every coincidence a synchronicity? The difference between the two lies in the term meaningful. Synchronicity is a coincidence with meaning or relevance.

★★★

★ ★ ★

When synchronicities occur, they're usually a surprise, precisely because they are unexpected events occurring outside of cause and effect.

★ ★ ★

time as meaning something more than mere chance, namely, a peculiar interdependence of objective events among themselves as well as with the subjective (psychic) states of the observer or observers."

While researching the phenomenon of the collective unconscious, Jung began to observe coincidences that were connected in such meaningful ways that their occurrence seemed to defy probability. In *The Structure and Dynamics of the Psyche*, he included examples culled from his case studies. Many of them are now legendary, including the following one:

"A young woman I was treating had, at a critical moment, a dream in which she was given a golden scarab. While she was telling me this dream I sat with my back to the closed window. Suddenly I heard a noise behind me, like a gentle tapping. I turned round and saw a flying insect knocking against the window-pane from outside. I opened the window and caught the creature in the air as it flew in. It was the nearest analogy to the golden scarab that one finds in our latitudes, a scarab beetle, the common rose-chafer (*Cetoaia urata*) which contrary to its usual habits had evidently felt an urge to get into a dark room at this particular moment. I must admit that nothing like it ever happened to me before or since, and that the dream of the patient has remained unique in my experience."

The Art of Divination

When synchronicities occur, they're usually a surprise, precisely because they are unexpected events occurring outside of cause and effect. But Carl Jung believed that we also could create synchronicity through the use of oracles or divination tools. While there are numerous forms of divination ranging from the casting of bones to the reading of tea leaves, Jung focused on the I Ching, the Tarot, and even astrology.

He considered the I Ching, a Chinese method of divination involving the tossing of yarrow sticks or coins, the clearest expression of the synchronicity principle: "The Chinese mind, as I see it at work in the I Ching, seems to be exclusively preoccupied with the chance aspect of events. What we call coincidence seems to be the chief concern of this peculiar mind, and what we worship as causality passes almost unnoticed...While the Western mind carefully sifts, weighs, selects, classifies, isolates, the Chinese picture of the moment encompasses everything down to the minutest nonsensical detail, because all of the ingredients make up the observed moment."

Likewise, Jung discovered that the synchronicity within the I Ching also extended to astrology. In a letter to Sigmund Freud dated June 12, 1911, he wrote: "My evenings are taken up largely with astrology. I make horoscopic calculations in order to find a clue to the core of psychological truth. Some remarkable things have turned up which will certainly appear incredible to you...I dare say that we shall one day discover in astrology a good deal of knowledge that has been intuitively projected into the heavens."

At the heart of Jung's concept of synchronicity is the belief in the ultimate oneness of the universe. As Jung put it, synchronicity suggests there is an interconnection or unity of causally unrelated events.

Deirdre Bair, author of *Jung: A Biography*, admits that synchronicity propelled her to write the book. After she'd written *Samuel Beckett: A Biography*, which won the National Book Award, she recalls, "Suddenly quite a lot of people who didn't know each other, and in several cases didn't know me either, were asking what my next book might be, and had I thought of writing about Jung?" Struck by the peculiar confluence of suggestions, Bair began researching the life and work of the famed psychiatrist.

Divination systems, such as the Tarot, the I Ching, and astrology, are complex and require substantial explanation. Some people spend years studying astrology, for instance, and still find new areas to explore. However, divination doesn't need to be complex. Here's a system you can practice with your morning cup of coffee, or with friends over coffee. It's adapted from *Café Nation: Coffee Folklore, Magick, and Divination* by Sandra Mizumoto Possey.

Exercise: A Simple Divination

All you need to begin is a cup of black coffee, a sugar cube, a spoon, and a question that you want answered. Choose any area of your life, such as love, finances, or career, and make sure that your question is open-ended, rather than one requiring a yes or no answer.

Clear your mind as you look into the blackness of the coffee. Focus on your question. As you continue gazing into the coffee, allow four possible answers or directions to come to mind. As thoughts come to you, make a mental note of them until you have reached four possible outcomes.

Next fill your spoon with coffee, holding it above the coffee cup. Now pick up your sugar cube and assign each of the lower corners one of the outcomes. Then place the cube in your spoon. The side that crumbles first represents the outcome with the most likelihood of happening, or the direction that will most likely be successful. If more than one corner collapses simultaneously, the outcome is yet to be determined, with possibilities lying between the two. The connection between the crumbling corner of the sugar cube and the best solution to your question is an example of divination, and an intentional synchronicity.

Compound Synchronicities

When one synchronistic event builds upon another, the idea that mere chance is the only explanation becomes even more unlikely. Take the following case involving two authors, both writing about synchronicity. UFO researcher Jacque Vallee was interested in a Los Angeles cult known as the Order of Melchizedec, related to an obscure biblical prophet named Melchizedec. He searched for information about the prophet, but didn't have much luck. In the midst of his research, he took a taxi to the Los Angeles airport and asked the taxi driver for a receipt. To his surprise, the receipt was signed "M. Melchizedec." He assumed the name must be more common than he thought, but when he checked the Los Angeles telephone directory, the only Melchizedec listed was his taxi driver.

Vallee offered a quirky explanation for how synchronicity works. He said it could be called "the angelic answer." Vallee suggested that it was as if he'd placed a message that read "Wanted: Melchizedecs" on a universal notice board. As a result, an earnest angel had asked, "How about this?" and handed Vallee the taxi driver.

To clarify his point, Vallee noted two ways a librarian could file information. One is alphabetical. But an easier way of filing would allow the librarian to place each new book on the closest shelf. Each book would have a beeper attached to its spine and could be located with a transmitter. Vallee proposed that the universe works on a similar system, and that explains synchronicity.

When the prolific writer Colin Wilson wrote about Vallee's theory for an article on synchronicity, he experienced a related synchronicity himself. After completing work on the passage about Vallee, Wilson took a break from writing to walk his dog.

As he left his office, he noticed that a book had fallen from a shelf. He picked it up and looked at the title, *You Are Sentenced to Life*, by Dr. W. D. Chesney. He'd bought it years ago, but had never read it. He paged through it and near the end found a page headed "Order of Melchizedec." It was a letter to the author by the founder of the order. Wilson noted that, of the more than 30,000 books in his house, it was that book which fell just after he had written about Melchizedec.

The Melchizedec tale reminded me of a somewhat similar event involving a name. While waiting for my car to be serviced at an auto dealer, I read an article on quantum physics in a copy of *Scientific American*. I noticed the name of a quantum physicist, Benjamin Schumacher. Just then the man behind the counter spoke loudly on the telephone saying, "Schumacher," which was the name of the dealer. I looked up and noticed a sign fifteen feet in front of me that said "Schumacher VW."

Exercise: Recalling Synchronicities

See if you can recall two synchronicities, one that happened to you long ago and another that occurred recently. Write them down in your notebook and create a title. Next try to recall the circumstances in more detail.

- ✪ Were you alone or with someone when the incident occurred?
- ✪ Were you thinking of something when an event occurred that related directly to your thoughts?
- ✪ Was it a chance meeting that led you to attaining something you desired?
- ✪ Were your surroundings well known to you or were they unfamiliar?

⭐ Were you talking about something unusual, such as some aspect of psychic phenomena?

⭐ How were you feeling when the synchronicity occurred?

That last question is significant. If you can identify a certain feeling that you associate with synchronicity, you can look for things to fall in place in unusual ways when you're feeling that way again.

Exercise: Programming Synchronicity

If you can't recall any synchronicities, or any recent ones, tell yourself that you will encounter a synchronistic event within the next twenty-four hours. It might be something minor, but pleasing. Perhaps just as you arrive at a crowded parking lot someone pulls out near the front. Perfect timing! You can even try creating that scenario by visualizing an empty parking place as you arrive and turn down one of the rows.

If you can identify a certain feeling that you associate with synchronicity, you can look for things to fall in place in unusual ways when you're feeling that way again.

Synchronicity Examples

Here's one example of a minor synchronicity that occurred to me while working on this chapter.

I was on my way to teach a private yoga class when I happened to glance at the sticker on the window that indicated the odometer reading for my next oil change. I then looked at the odometer to see how soon I would need an oil change. I was surprised to see that it read 46,206—the exact mile listed on the sticker!

Here's another example of synchronicity that happened to me years ago. It's more dramatic than the first example, both because of the emotions involved and because of the multiple layers of synchronicity.

I was driving on Interstate 95, taking two European visitors to the airport. We were deep in a discussion of spiritual concepts, and I was feeling lightheaded when I pointed out an odd license plate. It read "Zen 665." One of my passengers said, "Wouldn't it be something if we saw Zen 666?"

A few minutes later, still traveling on I-95, a car passed us with that very license plate. Even though we weren't talking about Zen or the meaning of 666, the astonishing synchronicity seemed related to the discussion. Years later, nearly a hundred miles away and long after the license plate would've expired, I spotted it again: Zen 666. This time I was alone and in a normal frame of mind. But the sight of the license plate served as a reminder of the earlier incident and the peculiar nature of that particular time.

Travel and Synchronicity

When you're traveling, you are removed from your regular routines. No matter how much you plan ahead, there are always surprises. The more you leave unplanned, the more fluid your journey. That opens the door for synchronistic events, such as the following one that I experienced while in Europe and North Africa years ago.

I was traveling with a friend, and one day we met an Australian named Maurey, who was traveling by himself. After that, we encountered Maurey repeatedly at hotels and restaurants as we journeyed across Spain. We didn't know where he was headed or when he was traveling, yet we managed to cross paths repeatedly. We stopped saying good-bye to him, because we figured we would probably see him again. While it could be said that we were all traveling on the same trail through Europe and foreign travelers tended to congregate in the same areas of cities, there were many others whom we met and never saw again.

Even less likely was an encounter with another friend who was traveling in Europe at the time. Dave supposedly was in Scandinavia. We didn't expect to see him and had no way of contacting him. We traveled farther south to the Mediterranean coast and boarded a ship leaving from the port city of Ceuta, Spain, for Morocco. We crossed the Strait of Gibraltar and docked in Tetouan. At the border, everything was confusing and chaotic. We were in a new country with a different language, culture, and customs. We passed through immigration and found a bus going to a small town in the mountains. Loud music was blasting from the driver's radio and several men wearing *jalabas*—long, hooded pullover robes—were arguing outside the bus. It all seemed very mysterious and disorienting.

We got on the crowded bus and found an empty seat. We noticed two other non-Arab men seated two rows in front of us. To our astonishment, one of them was our friend, Dave, who wasn't supposed to be anywhere near Morocco. As we greeted him, the man sitting next to him turned and calmly nodded to us. It was Maurey!

A Magician's Tale

Magicians are known for their tricks. Mentalists are magicians who feign psychic talents. Yet, there are some, such as David Blaine, who say their tricks are combined with actual psychic abilities. Here's a story he tells in his book, *Mysterious Stranger*, that combines tricks, psychic talent, and ultimately, synchronicity.

Blaine asked a woman to think of someone in her life who was important to her. After a moment, he said the name was short. He watched her body language closely and guessed that he was right. He sensed that it was someone close to her, then blurted, "The name symbolizes something else." He knew intuitively that he was right.

Just then a truck drove by with "White Rose," the name of a company, printed on the side. He sensed it was important. So he turned the woman around so she could see the truck and the name Rose. However, instead of looking at the truck, the woman's attention was drawn to a passing taxi with the word "DAWN" painted in large letters on the side. The woman screamed and broke down in tears. Dawn was the name of her mother, who had passed away, and the name she was thinking about.

"When it (coincidence) hits on this level, it seems to be more than a coincidence, as if there's some other force at work," Blaine writes.

Synchronicity and Precognition

In my research, I discovered that some authors blur the distinction between precognition and synchronicity. For example, when you suddenly think of someone from your past and that person appears in your life a short time later, is it precognition or synchronicity? Or is it both?

I was wondering about that question one day after reading two authors' descriptions of such a scenario. One called it precognition, the other synchronicity. An answer to my question came shortly. That evening, I happened to think of one of my yoga students who had moved away several months ago. I had no particular reason to think of her. While she had attended classes on a regular basis, I hadn't been particularly close to her. But, for some reason, I found myself wondering how she was doing. The next day a card arrived from her telling me exactly that.

I realized that it was a case of both precognition and synchronicity. It was *precognition* because I'd accurately sensed that she was about to contact me. However, it was a *synchronicity* because I'd experienced a scenario that was identical to the one I'd read about. Like the scenario the authors had described, I'd thought of someone not particularly close to me, then encountered the person, in this case, through a note in the mail.

Life as a Magical Play

As you read this chapter, you no doubt have noticed that I referred to synchronicities that occurred to me during my research, and these examples became part of the chapter. Meaningful coincidences abounded. It seemed that I would pick up a book and find exactly what I needed. Similar experiences occurred throughout the writing of the book. I was simply going with the flow. I was a player on a magical stage involved in the creation of a chapter and a book.

Of course, you don't have to be writing about synchronicity to experience it. No matter what you are doing, if you approach it as a play, you can experience synchronicity. In essence, you are the star of your own drama, and also an actor in a larger magical play that may be too large to completely grasp. That's synchronicity!

★ ★ ★

No matter what you are doing, if you approach it as a play, you can experience synchronicity.

★ ★ ★

5 Premonitions

In the science fiction movie *Minority Report*, three "precogs" float in an indoor swimming pool and project precognitive images onto a screen above them. Their directive is to pinpoint murders before they happen so that law officers of the Department of Pre-Crime can make an arrest before the murder is committed. It's an efficient program that, thanks to the precogs and their enhanced power of precognition, has cut the murder rate to zero in Washington, D.C., in the year 2054.

Is it possible to see into the future? If so, can we change the future? Research shows that the answer to both questions is yes. We can and do get glimpses of probable future events, but the future is not predestined. If we know what might happen, we can change circumstances and alter future events. For example, there are numerous reports of people foreseeing disasters, such as airplane crashes, and changing their plans, thus saving their lives and altering their futures.

While *Minority Report* is a work of fiction, the Central Premonitions Registry is not. It's a real register where anyone can report a precognitive dream. If a pattern appears with numerous people making the same prediction, such as an assassination attempt or a disaster, the people in charge of the registry will issue a warning in an attempt to change the future and prevent the predicted incident from occurring.

The Registry was created after a tragic coal mine collapse in the Welsh village of Aberfan killed 128 schoolchildren. Many people had accurate premonitions of that event. Such precognitive dreams are usually accompanied by a feeling of foreboding, a sense that danger is nearby.

Reporting a Premonition

If you want to report a dream of a disaster that you think might be a premonition, you can do so at the Web site of the Central Premonitions Registry at *www.mainportals.com/precog.shtml*. A form is provided. Respond as soon as possible since you may forget details or fail to act before the incident. Include everything you can remember, even if it seems trivial and of no significance. Such details may seem meaningless now, but they won't later.

So far the registry has not prevented any disaster from happening. Part of the reason is that premonitions and precognitive dreams, if they are accurate, usually come true within a few hours, or at most within a day or two. As a result, they are often reported after the event, which of course means they can't be used to prevent disasters.

There's another reason premonitions usually fail as a warning system. You might save yourself from a disaster, but don't count on others to heed your warning. Take the case of sixteen-year-old Carole Davis whose story was reported in *The Sense of Being Stared At* by Rupert Sheldrake. Carole was leaving a video arcade on a rainy night when she felt a terrible foreboding. As she paused near the crowded entrance where people were huddled to escape the sudden downpour, she glimpsed an image in her mind's eye that looked like a photograph of a disaster scene, with girders and tiles piled on people. She looked up and realized it was going to happen right there.

She yelled for everyone to get out of the way, but people just ignored her. She and her friends left for a nearby café where they soon heard the sound of sirens. They ran back to the arcade and saw a man being pulled from the wreckage of girders, just as she had foreseen.

9-11 Premonitions

In the aftermath of the World Trade Center disaster, Rupert Sheldrake, a biologist and psychic researcher, suspected that many people had premonitions about the terrorist attack. He placed a newspaper ad in the *Village Voice* and posters in Union Square in New York City, seeking dreams and premonitions about the tragedy. He received 57 responses; 38 involved precognitive dreams and 15 were related to premonitions.

About a third of the dreams occurred the night before the disaster and another third during the preceding five to six days. Sheldrake felt that the response represented only a fraction of the many people who probably experienced related premonitions. Several respondents dreamed of buildings collapsing, explosions in New York, airplanes crashing into buildings, or people running in panic. The most impressive premonitions were those by people who told others about them before the terrorist attack, and premonitions from people who rarely experienced such feelings of foreboding.

Mike Cherni, a forensic scientist who lives in New York City, dreamed of flying low over buildings he recognized in Manhattan. He and other passengers were upset. He felt an overwhelming sense of dread, then a tremendous impact, and that's when he woke up.

Amanda Bernsohn, who worked three blocks from the World Trade Center, didn't know why she couldn't stop crying the night of September 10. When she finally fell asleep, she dreamed not of the World Trade Center, but of Nazis taking over New York. She overslept for the first time since she'd started her job eight months earlier and was awakened by a call from a friend shortly after the first plane struck the North Tower.

Three weeks before the World Trade Center disaster, I visited Cassadaga, Florida, a quaint spiritualist community in the central part of the state. (See Chapter 11 for more on Cassadaga.) Most of the residents are mediums—psychics who believe they receive information through spirit guides—and I had a reading with one of them named Art Burley. I've forgotten much of what Art told me that day, but one image stands out. He said he saw two huge explosions coming: "I see them coming from above like huge bombs exploding. It's coming very soon. It's going to be very big, and it's going to change every-thing."

Art had been talking about my career and assumed the image was related to two big projects that would change my life. He knew I was a writer and speculated that it had some-thing to do with one of my novels being made into a movie. Put that way, it sounded good. But the image itself did not. While explosions can symbolize something spectacular, bombs in the creative world are bad news. And why was it coming from over-head? What did that mean?

I believe Art had inadvertently allowed his logic and reason-ing to interfere with the real message. He had tuned in to a truly dramatic, earth-shaking event that had a much larger scope than anything related to my career. If he'd avoided the all-too-common tendency to analyze the intuitive information, he might have realized that his guides were urgently sending out information about a major catastrophe on the horizon.

A famous case of a premonition that served as a life-and-death warning related to the actor James Dean. He was show-ing off his new Porsche to Alec Guinness when the writer/actor glimpsed Dean in an accident in the car. The impression was so startling to Guinness that he told Dean not to drive the car or he'd be dead in a week, he wrote in his autobiography. Dean, however, ignored the warning. A week later, he crashed the Porsche and died.

Poe Saw It Coming!

Sometimes spontaneous psychic experiences are entangled with the creative process. Take the case of Edgar Allan Poe, who in his unfinished sea-adventure novel, *The Narrative of Arthur Gordon Pym*, revealed something about his uncanny ability to penetrate into unknown realms.

In the story, there's an episode in which four men are ship-wrecked in an open boat. They're on the brink of starvation when the men draw lots to determine which one of them will be killed and eaten. Richard Parker, the cabin boy, draws the short straw, and he is promptly stabbed and devoured.

Gruesome as the tale is, the most astonishing thing about it is the fact that it reflected a future reality. Forty years after the story was written, a cabin boy named Richard Parker was actually killed and eaten in a remarkably similar incident. The four shipwrecked survivors were in an open boat and they drew straws to determine the victim. In the real-life incident, the men survived and stood trial for the boy's murder.

The incredible connection between fiction and real life was revealed years later when a twelve-year-old boy, who was related to Richard Parker, submitted the story to the *London Sunday Times* in a contest to find the best coincidence. The *Times* called it one of the most incredible "coincidences" ever recorded.

In *Shadow—A Parable*, Poe addresses readers of the distant future and seems to tell us that his stories contain such fasci-nating psychic connections. He writes: "Ye who read are still among the living, but I who write shall have long since gone my way into the region of shadows. For indeed strange things shall happen, and many secret things be known, and many centuries shall pass away, ere these memorials be seen of men. And, when seen, there will be some to disbelieve, and some to doubt, and yet a few who will find much to ponder upon in the characters here graven with a stylus of iron."

Titanic Disaster Foreseen

Disasters seem to generate latent psychic abilities. For example, just before the launching of the *Titanic* many people experienced ominous premonitions that the unsinkable ship would never reach America on its maiden journey from England. Some passengers, including Frank Adelman and his wife of Seattle, canceled their passage. Just as they were about to board the *Titanic*, Mrs. Adelman sensed danger and convinced her husband to postpone the trip.

Others who weren't passengers also reported foreboding premonitions about the *Titanic*. Blanche Marshall, who lived near Southampton, the launch site of the vessel, clutched her husband's arm as the *Titanic* left port and reportedly said, "That ship is going to sink before it reaches America." Her husband and others tried to calm her by saying that it was impossible. But Mrs. Marshall responded angrily, "Don't stand there staring at me. Do something! You fools, I can see hundreds of people struggling in the icy waters!"

Fourteen years before the launching of the *Titanic*, Morgan Robertson seemingly tuned into the disaster. In Robertson's novel, *Futility*, a cruise ship named the *Titan*, regarded as unsinkable, disappears after striking an iceberg, just as the *Titanic* would do. The dimensions of the ship and the number of passengers are similar to those of the *Titanic*. In Robertson's novel, the vessel sinks in April, the same month as the *Titanic*. There are 24 lifeboats on the fictional *Titan*, just four more than on the *Titanic*. In the story, the ship is traveling at 25 knots when it sinks; the *Titanic*'s speed was 22.5 knots.

Premonitions and precognitive dreams usually are personal in nature and concern events that are about to take place within a few hours or days.

The Prophecies of Nostradamus and Edgar Cayce

So what's the difference between a premonition and a prophecy? Premonitions and precognitive dreams usually are personal in nature and concern events that are about to take place within a few hours or days. Prophecy is about the big picture, often about major events in the distant future, and prophets are often associated with religion, especially the inception of a religion.

The prophecies of Nostradamus and Edgar Cayce, however, aren't associated with any particular religion. Nostradamus was born Michel de Nostredame in France in 1503. Of Jewish parents, he was forced by the Inquisition to convert to Catholicism. He became a skilled physician but would gain renown during his lifetime and far beyond as a seer of the future.

Nostradamus wrote his first set of one hundred prophecies, known as quatrains, when he was fifty-two years old. He wrote ten volumes of prophecies before his death, which he also predicted to the day. The problem with Nostradamus' prophecies is that they are written as metaphors and are open to a variety of interpretations. He covers five hundred years, right up to our times, but he rarely provides specific dates.

In one instance when he did provide a date, the prophecy was intriguing but the much-awaited date passed without any significant occurrence. Writing in the mid-sixteenth century, Nostradamus prophesied that the "King of Terror will come from the sky in the seventh month of 1999." Nothing notable happened that month, but two years and two months later, the terrorist, Osama bin Laden struck from the sky, destroying the twin towers of the World Trade Center. In 1999 and 2000, the prediction seemed wrong. But in the aftermath of 9/11,

Nostradamus, writing from the distant past, seems frighteningly accurate, if not precise on the date.

Edgar Cayce was a devout Christian whose prophecies, many of which related to the legendary island of Atlantis and reincarnation, baffled him because they contradicted his religious beliefs. He gave his readings, including prophecies for the future, while in a light trance with his eyes closed. He became known as the Sleeping Prophet. He said he never remembered what he said and had to read his own material to learn of his prophecies.

For forty-three years of his adult life, Cayce would lie down on a couch with his hands folded over his stomach and allow himself to enter a self-induced sleep state. In the 1920s, he first warned of coming racial strife in the United States, and in 1939 he predicted the deaths of two presidents in office: "Ye are to have turmoils — ye are to have strife between capital and labor. Ye are to have a division in thy own land, before ye have the second of the Presidents that next will not live through his office... a mob rule!" President Franklin D. Roosevelt died in office in April 1945. In November 1963, President John F. Kennedy was assassinated in Dallas, Texas, when racial tensions in the United States were at their height.

Cayce also predicted the First and Second World Wars, the independence of India, and the 1929 stock market crash. He foretold the creation of the State of Israel fifteen years before the event.

His most disturbing predictions, however, concern vast geographical upheavals that would result in the destruction of New York, the disappearance of most of Japan, and a cataclysmic change in Northern Europe. He said these events would happen by 1998, and fortunately, he was wrong. However, some scientists now say that a shift of the Earth's axis could cause dra-

matic changes in the weather, even climate changes, and it could happen any time.

Cayce's last prediction was much like the last one made by Nostradamus. On New Year's Day, 1945, Cayce announced that he would be buried on the fifth of January. He was right. Copies of more than 14,000 of Edgar Cayce's readings, including his prophecies, are available to the public at the Association for Research and Enlightenment (A.R.E.) in Virginia Beach, Virginia.

Are the Stories Proof?

In the world of science, premonitions, precognitive dreams, and prophecies are known as anecdotal evidence. Scientists may find tales of psychic power interesting, but even when they come true, they don't count them as proof of extrasensory perception. Even volumes of documented accounts with multiple witnesses wouldn't provide the proof scientists want. So how can precognition be tested?

Scientific Tests

In one test for precognition, the subject tries to guess the order of ESP or Zener cards before they are shuffled and turned over. Parapsychology laboratories have conducted such experiments since the 1930s. Initially, the cards were shuffled by hand; later automatic shuffling machines were used.

In the fifty-two years from 1935 to 1987, nearly two million trials were conducted with fifty thousand subjects. Dozens of different investigators were involved. Altogether, 309 studies were reported in 113 scientific articles. The results strongly supported the existence of precognition. When all the results were combined, they produced odds against chance of 10^{25} to 1. That's ten million billion billion to one. Something definitely was going on.

The Chair Test

Dutch psychic Gerard Croiset devised an experiment in which he would describe whoever sat in a randomly chosen chair at an upcoming public event. It didn't matter where the event was located as long as it took place within twenty-six days.

In one experiment, Croiset said that the person who would sit in the chair selected would be a man five feet nine inches tall, who brushed his black hair straight back, had a gold tooth in his lower jaw and a scar on his big toe, worked in both science and industry, and sometimes got his lab coat stained by a greenish chemical. Two weeks later a meeting took place in Denver and the person who sat down in the selected chair fit Croiset's description in every respect—except that he was five foot nine and three-quarters.

Croiset performed the chair test with repeated success over a twenty-five-year period. But sometimes he was wrong. The reason could relate to free will. In other words, although it seemed probable at the time of the experiment that the described person would sit in the chair, the individual changed his or her mind and didn't attend the event or chose another chair. Scientists were baffled by Croiset's successes, but skeptics maintained that it could be a clever trick and claimed there was room for cheating.

Test Your Precognition

Here's a chance to see if you have any precognitive dreams. The best time to try this experiment is a couple of days before going on a trip. The timing is important because you'll be able to identify the change from the usual setting of your life.

If you have trouble remembering dreams, you might read Chapter 9 before you attempt this exercise.

Exercise: Dreaming the Future

- ✪ Before going to bed, suggest to yourself that you'll have a dream of an upcoming event.
- ✪ Write down the dream images as soon as you wake up.
- ✪ Focus on the actual images. Don't try to interpret them.
- ✪ Pay attention to the scenery, the people, and the main incident.

Even if the details sound strange or crazy, write them down. They may not be so crazy when the incident actually occurs. Take a look at the following example.

A Silly Dream Comes True

Russell Targ, a physicist and co-founder of the Stanford Research Institute's investigation into psychic abilities in the 1970s and 1980s, recalls a precognitive dream he experienced while attending a scientific conference to present a technical paper. He dreamed that the person who was going to speak ahead of him wore a tuxedo with a red carnation in his lapel, and that he was going to sing his paper. The dream was striking in its clarity and bizarre nature, the sort of qualities that he associated with precognitive dreams.

The next morning on his way to breakfast he looked into the conference room to see what it looked like. To his astonishment, a man wearing a tuxedo with a red carnation on the lapel was standing near the lectern. He went up to him and asked him if he was going to sing. The man responded, "Yes, but not until later." It turned out he was a band leader and would be conducting at a banquet in the conference room later in the day.

Tapping into Your Psychic Abilities

In the next series of related exercises, you can test whether precognition is something you feel, glimpse, or hear. The methods, recommended by psychic researcher Pete A. Sanders Jr. in his book *You Are Psychic*, allow you to sample several different ways of accessing your psychic abilities. These methods are especially helpful because they provide a means of focusing your attention.

Whichever method you try, you first need to settle on a question related to a future event or a decision you will make. The more you desire to know the answer, the stronger your chances are to succeed. Begin each method by relaxing into your psychic power zone. Remember to take several deep breaths.

Exercise: Feeling the Future

✪ With your question in mind, phrase it in terms of your bodily sensations. In other words, "How do I feel about…"

✪ Become aware of the area between your solar plexus and your belly. What is your gut feeling about the question?

✪ Notice any sensations or emotions you experience. Is it a feeling of foreboding or danger, anger, or joy and elation? Is it a good feeling or a bad one? In what way? If you feel nothing, what kind of nothing is it? Is it a lack of something, something hidden, or nothing good?

✪ Jot down your feelings in the journal next to your question and interpret the meaning. If it's something you don't like, is there a way to change the circumstances to prevent that result?

There are numerous examples of people who have saved their lives by following their premonitions. . . . As you improve your abilities, learn to trust them.

★ ★ ★

Exercise: Seeing the Future

- ✪ Phrase your question in terms of vision, such as, "What do I see happening related to…"
- ✪ After relaxing, close your eyes and notice how the focus of your vision moves toward your forehead.
- ✪ Look for images to appear, like a movie in your mind.
- ✪ Jot down the images that appear to you, even if they don't seem to relate to your question. Look for anything symbolic, as if the images were a dream. See how they can be interpreted.

Exercise: Hearing the Future

- ✪ Keeping your question in mind, relate it to hearing. For example, "What do I hear related to…"
- ✪ After relaxing into a meditative state, close your eyes and listen. Cut out any traffic sounds or other distracting noises.
- ✪ Image a voice whispering in your ear. Listen for a message.
- ✪ Jot down whatever you hear, even if the message doesn't seem related to your question. Look for ways to apply the message to your question.

Powering Up

There are numerous examples of people who have saved their lives by following their premonitions. They avoided boarding an airplane that later crashed. They changed their plans to elude potential problems they sensed. As you improve your abilities, learn to trust them. Pay attention and act in the most appropriate manner to avoid or change the outcome, if it's one that you don't want to experience.

But should you warn others of potential danger? Although strangers and even friends won't necessarily pay attention to a warning based on a premonition, it's always worth mentioning it. But act with appropriate caution. Don't shout "fire" in a crowded room when there's no fire, even if you just saw one in your mind's eye. That could create a disaster. Instead, tell your friends you're uncomfortable and want to leave. You think something bad could happen. Remind them of any other instance when you perceived danger.

Beyond foreseeing disasters, your precognitive skills can aid you in your daily life, guiding you to make the right decisions.

6 Remote Viewing

*H*ave you ever wished that you could be at a certain place at a specific time and see what was going on without anyone knowing you were there? Actually, at one time or another, most of us have wanted to be the proverbial fly on the wall, the invisible observer. Wishful thinking? Not necessarily.

Remote viewing is a psychic skill that allows you to project a part of your mind elsewhere. It's an extrasensory talent that, once learned, allows you to see something that's well out of range of your normal vision. The term might sound as if it has something to do with the remote control of your television, but actually it was popularized through revelations about the U.S. military's use of psychic spies. More about the spy stuff later.

Besides remote viewing, it's also known by the French word *clairvoyance*, which means "clear seeing" or second sight. Other names for the talent are *remote perception* and *farseeing*. But how is this ability possible? How could anyone see something going on around the corner, across town, in another state, or even in another country without being there? Well, you could watch it on television, right?

Sure, but what if there were no television cameras present? You might get 150 channels, but that certainly won't help you find out what's going on at a friend's house tonight, and you won't find a lost watch by turning on the TV, either. Likewise, there is no cable channel that will tell you what's inside a sealed envelope or box, or where someone is hiding. Those are just a few examples of the things you can do when you learn the skill of remote viewing.

But back to that question: How is it possible? While your brain is the physical receptor of information, the mind exists beyond the physical limitations of the body. And, whether you

know it or not, you can send your mind elsewhere to gather information. Actually, you do it all the time when you're sleeping. But that's a topic for another chapter.

It might turn out that, after you've tested your skills with the help of a friend or two, you find out that you're a remote viewing genius, a psychic wunderkind! Or, you might have modest abilities. If you can't "see" anything in the experiments, it just means that you haven't practiced enough. Research has shown that *everyone*, with practice, can attain some degree of ability to far-see.

Spontaneous Remote Viewing

While learning to remote view can take time and practice, sometimes it just happens. Here's a case of spontaneous remote viewing recorded by Bernard Gittelson in *Intangible Evidence*.

A woman on an Oregon farm was jolted awake one morning at 3:40 A.M. by the sound of people screaming. The sound quickly vanished, but she felt a smoky, unpleasant taste in her mouth. She woke her husband, and together they scoured the farm but found nothing out of the ordinary. That evening on a television newscast, they heard about a plant explosion that started a huge chemical fire that killed six people. The explosion had occurred at 3:40 A.M.

A similar spontaneous remote viewing experience involving a fire came to Emmanuel Swedenborg, a scientist and inventor, in 1759. In Swedenborg's case, he "saw" a great fire raging in Stockholm, Sweden, and described it in detail to his guests in Gothenburg, 300 miles away. Later, the fire was confirmed. Since there were no telephones or televisions—or any kind of electronic communication—in Swedenborg's time, such an

Psychic power, including remote viewing, is our heritage, and with practice we can recapture the talent and enhance our natural abilities.

ability, whether spontaneous or programmed, was definitely a valuable and helpful skill.

An Ancient Skill

There's a theory that prehistoric people were able to survive their harsh environment because they possessed highly developed psychic skills, such as remote viewing. According to the theory, we gradually lost these abilities as civilization became more complex. The skills still exist, but at a much weaker level. Rather than using our inner resources, we tend to rely on technology. Instead of seeing distant events, such as dramatic fires, with our minds, we watch such events unfold on television, read about it on the Internet, or someone calls us on the telephone with the news.

Take the example of the Bogi people, who live on islands in Indonesia and are gifted builders of large wooden seagoing vessels. You might not know much about the Bogis, but you've probably heard of the bogeyman, right? That's because English explorers who ventured to Indonesia in the nineteenth century returned home with stories of the Bogis that fascinated and frightened their children.

But the Bogis are far more than caricatures for scary stories. For centuries, they sailed far out to sea in their boats without using any type of navigational equipment. Their shamans—healers with psychic abilities—were able to project their minds out to sea and locate other islands to which they sailed. While there are still Bogis who maintain this remote viewing skill, many now rely on compasses and other modern navigational equipment.

Psychic power, including remote viewing, is our heritage, and with practice we can recapture the talent and enhance our natural abilities. While technology has duplicated much of what remote viewing is about, there are still many aspects of the skill that technology can't imitate. For example, our electronic wizardry can't find a missing child. Information about the child can be disseminated instantly through the electronic media in the hope that someone will recognize the child, but someone capable of remote viewing might describe the child's actual location. The talent is also used to help track down criminals, find oil or minerals, discover unknown archaeological sites, and even diagnose medical conditions that puzzle the experts. Then, there's also the controversial military application—spying on enemy targets.

Remote Viewing Research

Serious scientific research into remote viewing, or clairvoyance, began in 1973 at the Stanford Research Institute in Menlo Park, California, under the direction of Harold Putoff and Russell Targ. The early experiments involved a highly sensitive psychic researcher named Ingo Swann. At first, they asked Swann to describe objects that were placed in another room. But when Swann became bored with the repetitive tasks, he created a new challenge.

He asked Putoff and Targ to give him map coordinates and see if he could describe the location. One of the most interesting results occurred when a skeptical scientist on the East Coast submitted coordinates. This is what Swann said, according to the laboratory transcripts:

This seems to be some sort of mounds or rolling hills. There is a city to the north; I can see taller buildings and some smog. This seems to be a strange place, somewhat like the lawns one would find around a military base, but I get the impression that either there are some old bunkers around or maybe this is a covered reservoir. There must be a flagpole, some highways to the west, possibly a river over to the far east, to the south more city...There is something strange about this area, but since I don't know what to look for within the scope of the cloudy ability, it is extremely difficult to make decisions on what is there and what is not. Imagination seems to get in the way. For example, I get the impression of something underground, but I'm not sure.

Swann also drew a picture of the image he'd seen. The transcript and picture were mailed to the scientist, who called back upon receiving it. The target was an underground missile site. Swann's description was correct in every detail and his drawing was accurate, even to scale.

Another example involved college students who were taking a test. Attached to each examination was a sealed envelope, and none of the students knew what was inside. Half of the envelopes contained the correct answers to the test. The other half contained only a few correct answers. The students took their exams without opening the envelopes. Interestingly, those who had envelopes with the correct answers performed better on the test than the other students. The students apparently used their psychic abilities, even though they weren't aware of it.

Psi Spies

As a result of the success rate of the experiments at the Stanford Research Institute, the U.S. government started taking an interest in the research. By the late 1970s, the CIA and the U.S. Army began training psychics for spying, a program that lasted twenty years. Although the program, known as Stargate, no longer exists, some government agencies may be using psychics on a project-by-project basis.

This practice was depicted in the popular television series *Dead Zone*, in an episode called "The Hunt for Osama." A team of psychic spies, working with the U.S. military, is joined by

John Smith, the show's main character, whose awesome psychic abilities are the result of a car accident that left him in a coma for six years. Interestingly, the story concept for the episode was created by Joseph McMoneagle, a former real-life psychic spy. McMoneagle, a chief warrant officer, learned the technique of remote viewing in the U.S. Army. He was the most talented and successful operative in the Stargate program. Known as Remote Viewer #001, he joined the program in 1978 and stayed with it until it ended in 1994.

Jim Schnabel, author of *Remote Viewers: The Secret History of America's Psychic Spies*, relates how, in one instance, McMoneagle was given an envelope with a picture inside and was told only that it was a person. He was given several dates and times and asked to describe the person and his surroundings at each time. He proceeded to describe a man dressed in a business suit with dark hair. He was driving a car through hilly countryside. About five minutes into the session, McMoneagle abruptly stopped and said he couldn't go any further. He said it was as if the picture of the man turned sideways and disappeared. He couldn't follow the man, he explained, because he couldn't go where the man went.

Later, McMoneagle found out that the man in question was a foreign agent who had failed to appear at a meeting and disappeared. But the mystery was solved when it was learned that he died in a car accident. During the time frame that McMoneagle had used in his session, the man had driven his car over a cliff, while speeding along a winding road in Italy.

In another case, cited by Dean Radin in *The Conscious Universe*, McMoneagle was given only the map coordinates of a big building in Russia in which some sort of secret construction project was taking place. When he accurately drew the building and its surroundings, he was given a photo of it and asked what was inside. He described in detail the construction of an enormous submarine, larger than any in existence. Staff members of the National Security Council, which had asked for his help, didn't believe it was true, especially since the warehouse was located one hundred yards from the water and no one seemed to know anything about such a project. McMoneagle said the vessel would be launched in four months. Spy photographs later showed the Russians using explosives to create a canal to the warehouse through which the largest submarine ever seen was launched. It happened four months after McMoneagle's remote viewing session.

In May 2004, I asked Joe McMoneagle to remote view a target for me. He was kind enough to agree to my request. The target was an aerial photo of a secret Navy base, known as AUTEC, Atlantic Underwater Test and Evaluation Center, located on Andros Island in the Bahamas. According to the AUTEC Web site, the base includes a secret underwater submarine dock that is nearly the size of the base's land area. The site states that "AUTEC's vision is to be the Department of Defense and Navy range of choice for conducting undersea warfare testing and measurements in the Atlantic."

The photo had been taken a month earlier by a pilot who received permission to fly over the base. Following the guidelines provided by McMoneagle's wife, Nancy, I sealed the photo in an envelope. On the outside of the envelope, Nancy wrote "Target #BG5406" and the simple direction "Describe purpose of target."

McMoneagle described a collection of "small single-level buildings," and provided far more detail than was visible from the photo: "There is a very exotic ground-plane system and electronic frequency-tuning system involved here, as well as some sort of a sophisticated monitoring system emplaced which is in twenty-four-hour operation. I'm also getting a very strong sensitivity feeling…not sensitive in the sense of electronics, but sensitive in the sense of security. These systems are associated with Special Access programs and Darkened [top secret] projects, as well as high level security systems attached to or having to do with submarine communications, tracking, and identifications."

McMoneagle concluded: "This is a down-range weather station and communications relay for Cape Canaveral co-located with probably a United States Naval Base, doing some sort of submarine communications relay, tracking, and identification. The location given the antenna field and stylization of buildings, vehicles, people, smells, air, layout, etc. would be Bahamas (80%), Turks and Caicos (50%), Virgin Islands (30%), and Leeward Islands (15%)."

The envelope was later returned to me with my seal still intact. For all McMoneagle knew, it could have contained a picture of my dog. Instead, it was a photograph of the base. Even though Stargate ended a decade ago, McMoneagle, it seems, is still Remote Viewer #001.

What It Takes

So that's the sort of thing that psychic spies do. But what can you do? Before you dive into remote viewing, you need to prepare yourself. Here are a few general guidelines.

1) Keep in mind that you have psychic abilities. You are capable of remote viewing. It's all about listening to your inner voice and using your inner vision. Once you recognize that voice and pay attention to it, it will become easier to get answers to your questions and find whatever you are seeking.

Keep in mind that you have psychic abilities. You are capable of remote viewing. It's all about listening to your inner voice and using your inner vision.

2) You are entitled to psychic power. Don't be afraid of the talent or ashamed of being psychic. Some people are concerned that their friends might think they're freaks or kooks. The truth is that developing intuitive skills, such as remote viewing, can benefit you throughout your life in ways that you can't yet imagine.

3) Take an active role. Don't wait for a remote viewing incident to happen spontaneously. Go for it. Make an effort. The best way to understand what it's about is to experience it firsthand. Reading about it only goes so far, and wishing won't make it happen. Make a determined effort and you'll get results.

4) Learn to distinguish between the mind's idle chatter— your internal dialogue with yourself—and psychic functioning, which usually manifests itself as subtle, fleeting messages or images that come to mind when you quiet the inevitable chatter.

5) Be skeptical about information that comes to you in great detail, especially when you're just beginning. That usually means that you are analyzing your impression and dressing it up. For example, if you see several inverted Vs stacked one on top of another, you might call it a pine tree because that's what it reminds you of. But it could relate to something entirely different, such as the design on the front of a building. So stick with your first impression and don't try to figure it out.

6) Find a friend or two interested in remote viewing. By making it a group activity, you have others to talk to about the results and it makes for better experiments, as you'll see.

Getting Ready

Now let's get more specific. Let's say you're ready to try one of the experiments and you have a partner or two on hand to help out. Here are some pointers for preparing yourself.

1) Find a private and quiet place to work where you won't be interrupted. You don't want to be disturbed by family members.

2) Find a comfortable chair.

3) Use the bathroom, if necessary.

4) Eat something, if you're hungry, but not too much.

5) Check your emotions. Are you calm and relaxed? If there's something upsetting or angering you, hold off until you're more centered.

6) Let go of everything outside of the room. Your concerns and worries will wait for you, if you want them back. Stay right in the present moment as you prepare yourself for the session.

7) Make sure there are no pets present. A cat hopping on your lap can ruin a session.

8) Turn off any cell phones. Unplug any other phones in the room.

9) Make sure that your writing tools are handy and you have a convenient place to write or draw, such as a desk or table.

10) Pull the blinds or lower the light level to create a more conducive environment for remote viewing.

11) You need to relax and to focus your mind before you begin remote viewing. Both techniques are described in Chapter 2. By now, if you've practiced, you should know how you feel when you enter a relaxed state.

Exercise: Remote Viewing an Object

So now you're ready to start. This exercise is derived from the laboratory testing program that was used at the Stanford Research Institute and is a good one for your first attempt at remote viewing. You need at least one friend, but two are preferable, one to hide the object and one to interview you. If you have only one helper, eliminate the interviewer.

Your mission in this exercise is to describe an object, then identify it using your psychic power. In another room, your assistant will choose a small object and place it in a bag, a box, or an envelope so that you cannot possibly know what it is. The best objects are things that have several sensory details. A piece of sandpaper, for example, would have color, texture, and sound attached to it. A tomato would have scent, color, texture, and shape. Your friend must stay there with the object, so as not give you (or the interviewer) any clues about its identity. From the minute the object is placed in the bag, you should close your eyes and begin to write down or tape-record your impressions. You also can draw the object.

If no impressions come to mind, here are a couple of methods you might try. Tell yourself to look into the future and see the object being placed in your hand at the end of the exercise. Alternately, look into the past before it was placed in the bag. Use all your senses: see it, feel it, smell it, taste it. Do not try to guess what it is; let your impressions and the sensory information accumulate.

Meanwhile, if a second friend is on hand, he or she should ask you questions that guide you to new ways of experiencing the object and keep you from getting off track. For example, if you are describing a round, red object, the interviewer might ask you its texture. Is it smooth or hard? You might also be asked to look at the object from a different angle. Make sure that the interviewer doesn't know the identity of the object. You don't want leading questions that will taint the results.

Stop when you run out of impressions. Set a time limit of ten or fifteen minutes—any longer isn't necessary for a simple object. At this point, your friend should bring you the object and you should hold it in your hands. Feel it and sense all its qualities. Make a mental note of which characteristics came through clearly and which ones were muted or missing altogether. Notice whether you got sidetracked by the tendency to overanalyze. Don't skip this final step—it is important feedback in the process of learning the skill of remote viewing.

Exercise: Remote Viewing a Location

This exercise was also derived from the work at the Stanford Research Institute. It's similar to the first one, except this time you're going to attempt to describe a location. You'll begin your remote viewing at the same time that your helper arrives at the location.

Ask a friend to go to a specific place of his or her choice. Make sure that it's not an obvious place, such as a national monument located nearby. Your friend should arrive at a specific time and spend about fifteen minutes there. She should look around, focusing on tall things or angular objects, soft things and sharp things. Your friend should be aware of sounds, smells, and movement. She should look, but avoid making any effort to send you any information.

As the appointed time approaches, you should prepare yourself by finding a comfortable and quiet place to conduct your mission. Relax and stay calm. Don't forget to take several deep breaths. Then, as the time frame begins, start to describe your impressions. You might want to have another friend, who doesn't know where the helper has gone, ask you questions. Describe all the qualities that you sense—the shapes and sizes, the colors and textures, the scents and movement.

Look at the site from several angles. Try to hover above it. Look, but don't analyze. If you want, sketch the scene as well as describing it in writing.

When the time is up, your friend should call or e-mail you with the location and a description. Visit the place as soon as you can and look for things that resemble the images you saw.

Whether you are remote viewing an object or a location, don't be surprised if you get information that is totally irrelevant. That's just your mind's chatter getting in the way or your attempt to analyze rather than see. With practice, you'll be able to separate the good information from the rest. If you take turns being the viewer with your friends, you'll soon see how others tend to analyze and how that process distorts the original impression.

Exercise: Remote Viewing the Future

This exercise is identical to the previous one, with two important exceptions. First, your friend who will go to the target should avoid selecting it in advance. Instead, he should locate a target within a few minutes of the established beginning time. Back at your home base, you should begin the session at least fifteen minutes before your friend selects the target. In other words, you are remote viewing the location where your subject will be at a particular time in the future.

By asking you to describe the future location of your friend, this exercise eliminates the possibility that telepathy is involved. That's because your friend hasn't selected the target when you describe it.

Putting Remote Viewing to Use

Don't get frustrated if your efforts fail at first in any of these exercises. Some people are naturals. Others require more practice. But if you make the effort, you'll eventually pick up images and get results. When you do, you'll gain a new sense of power—psychic power. You can do it and you'll get better with experience.

While you need to practice and experiment, think about your ability as something that can be put to good use as well as play. Sooner or later, you'll encounter a real-life situation in which you can call on your psychic power. It could be something simple, like finding a lost watch or missing car keys. It might also be something more serious, like locating a lost pet or even a missing child. Whatever the circumstances, you can challenge yourself by moving from the experimental into the practical. You'll then fully realize that developing psychic power is not just a game or hobby, but a skill that can be used to help yourself and others.

7 Hands-On Psi

When psychic Johnny Smith shakes hands with a congressional candidate named Greg Stillson, he glimpses images of a nuclear holocaust, Armageddon—the end of the world as we know it—and he realizes that Stillson will be behind the devastation. Now, even though he has no evidence, he must stop Stillson.

That's the ongoing theme of the television series *Dead Zone*, in which Anthony Michael Hall plays Johnny Smith. Smith's psychic power, known as psychometry, is at the heart of series. Whatever Smith touches plays a role in solving a crime or unraveling a mystery.

Psychometry, essentially, is the ability to read the thoughts that impregnate an object. It's hands-on psychic power, or psychic touch.

Origins

If you find the formal term confusing—it sounds like a cross between psychology and geometry—you can blame a man named Joseph Rhodes Buchanan. He was an American physiologist who coined the term in the mid-nineteenth century. The word is derived from two Greek words, *psyche,* meaning "the soul," and *metro,* indicating a "measure." Hence, *psychometry,* by this definition, means the power to measure and interpret the soul of things.

Buchanan claimed that he could determine the soul or nature of all things through touch. He believed that the past was entombed in the present and could be deciphered through this psychic ability. Keep in mind that while Buchanan studied and named the ability, psychic touch, like other forms of psychic power, has been woven into the fabric of humanity since ancient times.

Born in 1815, Buchanan was a child prodigy. He studied geometry and astronomy at the age of six. By the age of twelve, he began studying law. While in his teens, he became a teacher, and he soon became fascinated by the works of Franz Mesmer, who thought the universe was permeated by magnetic fluid that affects our well-being. His interest in psychic touch developed after he met an Episcopalian bishop who told him that he could distinguish brass in the dark from other metals because it left a disagreeable taste in his mouth when he touched it. Soon Buchanan was exploring the outer boundaries of the sense of touch. He found that many of his subjects in experiments could determine salt, pepper, sugar, and vinegar by feeling them. Buchanan didn't find the ability extrasensory at all. If the tongue could determine these substances, why couldn't the fingertips?

But when Buchanan expanded to areas beyond such sub-stances, he realized that he was dealing with extrasensory touch and not a variation of the sense of taste. For example, he provided his best subjects with letters written with strong emo-tions, and many were able to describe the nature of the feelings projected by the letter writer simply by holding the folded letter. Some of Buchanan's subjects also touched people and suppos-edly were able to accurately describe their emotional states and physical conditions.

While Buchanan dabbled with the use of psychometry in healing, he enthusiastically championed the use of psychic power in the study of the distant past. In his "Original Sketch" describing psychometry, written in 1848, he said:

"If, then, man in every act, leaves the impression or daguerreotype of his mental being upon the scenes of his life and subjects of his action, we are by this law furnished with a new clue to the history of our race; and I think it highly probable that, by the application of this principle, the chasms of history may be supplied, and a glimpse may be obtained of unrecorded ages and nations whose early history is lost in darkness."

He continued, adding more detail: "The ancient manuscripts, paintings and other works of art...are doubtless still instinct with the spirit that produced them, and capable of revealing to psychometric exploration the living realities with which they were once connected."

Years later, some researchers, archaeologists, and adventurers took up the challenge.

Psychic Archaeology

An Englishman named William Denton, a contemporary of Buchanan's, was the first researcher to use psychometrists to study the past. In his book, *The Soul of Things,* he includes numerous examples of successful efforts to view the past through psychic touch.

- ✪ A stone fragment from the Porcelain Tower near Peking resulted in an accurate description of a temple with massive walls and large urns, a bell-shaped roof and a spire.
- ✪ A piece of limestone slab from Nineveh garnered an impression of a vast temple.
- ✪ A Greek coin that was held but hidden from view brought a detailed description of the mint where it was created.
- ✪ A piece of curtain from the U.S. House of Representatives translated to a large council chamber, and an impression of some members talking in a superficial manner.
- ✪ A piece of sandstone from Melrose Abbey in Scotland led to a description of an abbey with arched doorways, Gothic windows, and an aisle.

One of the best psychometrists was Denton's wife. In one test, Denton gave her a piece of lava the size of a bean that came from Pompeii. She could hold it, but she wasn't allowed to see it. Mrs. Denton saw colored figures painted on a wall—frescoes—of a building that overlooked the sea. Through the window, she saw smoke and cinders rising from a mountaintop. A black cloud of dust was spreading across the countryside. Mrs. Denton said, "I feel the influence of human terror that I cannot describe."

Colonel Percy Harrison Fawcett, an English adventurer who searched for a lost city in the Amazon and disappeared in the 1920s, believed that information could be obtained from objects through touch. Fawcett possessed a black basalt stone idol, given to him by Sir H. Rider Haggard. Fawcett wrote, "I could think of only one way of learning the secret of the stone image, and that was by means of psychometry—a method that may evoke scorn by many people but is widely accepted by others who have managed to keep their minds free from prejudice."

In *Lost Trails, Lost Cities*, Fawcett tells of handing the idol to a psychometrist, who described "a large irregularly shaped continent stretching from the north coast of Africa across to South America. The psychometrist continued: "I see volcanoes in violent eruptions, flaming lava pouring down their sides, and the whole land shakes with a mighty rumbling sound... A voice says: 'The judgment of Atlanta will be the fate of all who presume to deific power!' I can get no definite date of the catastrophe, but it was long prior to the rise of Egypt, and has been forgotten—except, perhaps, in myth." Fawcett asserted that "the connection of Atlantis with parts of what is now Brazil is not to be dismissed contemptuously, and belief in it—with or without scientific corroboration—affords explanations for many problems which otherwise are unsolved mysteries."

Psychic Criminology

While Johnny Smith, the psychometrist in *Dead Zone*, is a fictional character, psychics with his abilities are sometimes called into criminal investigations and searches for missing people. One such real-life psychometrist was Renie Wiley, who died in 2002. The daughter of the first woman to graduate from the Florida Police Academy, Wiley was at ease in working with law enforcement officers. She even led workshops in South Florida to help cops tune into their own psychic power. She knew their language and usually talked about gut feelings or hunches rather than intuition or psychic abilities.

After reading a newspaper article about Renie Wiley, I met her and accompanied her on an investigation for an article called "The Psychic vs. the Killer" that was published in the July 1984 issue of *Fate* magazine. The case, which involved the murder of a young woman at an exclusive country club, provided a dramatic exhibition of psychometry.

Police were unable to solve the case and several months after the murder, Wiley's assistance was requested. At the police station, Wiley held a photo of the victim, then began sketching the face of the man she said was the killer. Her skills as a commercial artist helped her create detailed features. She felt there was a uniform involved—a policeman, security guard, maybe a soldier. One of the detectives said he recognized the face as someone who'd been at the scene the night of the murder, but wasn't accused of committing the crime.

The plan was to take Wiley to the woman's apartment and let her hold objects owned by the victim to see what information she could gather. However, as soon as they arrived at the complex, Wiley began tuning into the murder. When they parked in an underground lot, the detective asked Wiley where the murder was committed. Without hesitating, she pointed to a door; the detective glanced at his partner and they both nodded, acknowledging that she was right.

Psychic Touch and Empathy

As soon as she got out of the car, Wiley slipped off her shoes and went to work. Besides using psychic touch, Wiley was an empath, someone who felt and experienced the emotions of other people. Not only was she able to empathize with those involved in a crime, but she seemingly could enter the time frame in which the event took place. She called it "bird dogging."

"When I bird-dog, I don't know what I'm doing or where I'm going," she explained. "I usually can't talk because I'm not in control. I've got to be either barefoot or wearing soft-soled shoes like moccasins, so I can feel the ground."

She took several deep breaths, then explained that she was tuning into the woman before her death: "I see her carrying something, a bulky brown object. She was taking it into the storage room near her parking spot." She saw the woman entering the storage room and being surprised by her attacker. The object was knocked out of her arms, and the man stabbed her in the stomach so violently that the blow severed her spinal cord. She fell over a bicycle and died instantly.

The two detectives confirmed her reconstruction of the crime, including the severity of the wound. They also told Wiley that the bulky brown object was a brown beanbag chair. When they led Wiley upstairs to the young woman's apartment, she walked directly to the bedroom, found a teddy bear and hugged it. "I was in her head then," she said, "picking up things about her personal life. There was a lot of depression, sadness." She stopped in front of a sliding glass door, rocking back and forth with the teddy bear in her arms, gazing out at the golf course. "There was something about it which disturbed me, frightened me. I don't know what," Wiley recalled.

Once she was back at the station, Wiley related that she felt the woman had stumbled onto a drug deal when she entered the garage area. Three men were involved—the murderer, whom she had sketched, and two witnesses. One of the detectives handed Wiley a piece of the door from the garage. It was stained with the victim's blood. "What are you getting from that?" he asked.

She didn't respond. She didn't move. Her eyes were glazed. "I immediately went into trauma," she later recalled. "All of a sudden I was no longer at the police station. I was in the garage again, in the murderer's head." After a minute, she turned to the detective and told him to take her back to the building.

As soon as they got there, Wiley bounded out of the car and ran between two buildings. Her shoes were off and she was running hard, picking up impressions. "I was looking for water," she said. "I kept hearing a trickle of water in my left ear. That told me I had to go left. I was getting landmarks, seeing what he saw." She passed a pond and when she reached the next building, she stopped in front of a garage. Her fists clenched and her breathing pattern changed. Although the detectives hadn't lost sight of her, Wiley said she had entered the time just after the murder: "I knew he was just behind the door and I was afraid to open it. I was afraid I might be manifested—in his time—and that I'd be in danger." She backed into one of the detectives and was catapulted into the present. The detective opened the door, revealing a dumpster with a chute over it that connected to various floors of the building. "The murder weapon was hidden up there," she said. "He ran to this building and hid it. Later, he came back for it."

At that point, Wiley said she wanted nothing more to do with the case. She felt that one of the witnesses had been watching them and she sensed her own life was in danger. She was clearly frightened and also asked me not to write anything about it. (Later, she changed her mind and said it was okay as long as I didn't use the name of the victim and obscured some of the details. The detectives also didn't want their names used.)

As they were leaving the complex, she pointed to a building. "There's something about that building. I think he lives there," she said. The detective looked stunned and replied, "Now you're picking up my other case." Residing in the building was a man believed to be one of the largest drug dealers in South Florida.

A short time later, a security guard at the complex, the man Wiley had sketched, was arrested and convicted of first-degree murder. The two witnesses were never identified. No evidence was found linking the suspected drug dealer to the case. Wiley, however, remained concerned about her safety until she moved to Colorado a few years after the murder.

Renie Wiley's experience is an extreme example of psychometry. Chances are you won't be catapulted into another time or find yourself in any danger. Psychic touch, in fact, is a challenging ability to learn. But with practice, you can pick up impressions from an object that can lead you into its past. Here's how to begin.

Psychic touch, in fact, is a challenging ability to learn. But with practice, you can pick up impressions from an object that can lead you into its past.

Exercise: Are You a Psychometrist?

You probably have some psychometric abilities, even though you may not know it. Answer these questions to find out:

✪ Have you ever sensed someone staring at you, or felt someone's presence in a room before you knew anyone was there?

✪ Do you get strong feelings, a flood of emotions and memories, when you look at old photographs?

✪ When you touch another person or shake someone's hand, do you get impressions about the person's personality?

✪ Have you ever entered a room and sensed that an argument had just taken place?

✪ Do you sense other people's moods and adapt to them as if they were your own?

Exercise: Getting in Touch

If you answered positively to one or more of the above questions, then you may have some psychometric abilities. Of course, the only way to find out is to try it.

Start with familiar objects, such as a family member's watch or ring, or maybe a brooch that your grandmother wore. You could also use an article of clothing or a letter from a friend.

Find a quiet place where you can relax and clear your mind. Remember to take several deep breaths. Keep a positive attitude. Tell yourself that you can do it. Trust your abilities.

Hold the object between your hands. You also might try holding it to your forehead to the "third eye." You may find it hard to distinguish what you already know about the person from what you are obtaining from the object. If you sense something that you didn't know about the person, see if you can find out if it's true.

If you're having trouble getting impressions, don't try so hard. Relax, and as your mind starts to drift, note any stray impressions, visual or auditory, that touch the edge of your consciousness. Follow whatever it is, see where it takes you.

Next, work with objects with unfamiliar connections. It could be a folded letter that's not addressed to you and that you haven't read. You might work with something from the distant past, such as a piece of pottery or an arrowhead. Sometimes you can pick up information about a time or place or people that can be verified. Other times, if it's more personalized information, you have to trust your feelings. Here's an example.

As I was researching psychometry, I tried my hand at it, so to speak. I picked up a pottery chip from a basket on my bookshelf. I'd found it in Utah near the Four Corners, a region once inhabited by the Anasazis. After holding it a couple of minutes, I sensed flowing water. Next, I glimpsed a teenage girl and realized she was crouched by a river or stream. She was involved with some activity there, possibly washing clothes. But she was continually distracted by younger children nearby. She was laughing, enjoying herself.

Maybe it was all my imagination, I thought. After all, I write fiction and have an active imagination. But then I noticed that the girl kept looking up, somewhat apprehensive. Was she worried about rain in the desert? Then I sensed a high wall of rock nearby jutting skyward. She was looking up at people living on the rock wall—cliff dwellers. She was thinking that someone was waiting for her, maybe getting impatient.

Such a scenario would be hard to prove. Yet, it felt as if the girl was acting on her own, that I was picking up something from the past imbedded in the pottery.

Psychometry at Work

Here's a case where a psychometrist's impressions were verified. One of the best psychics of the twentieth century was Eileen Garrett, who worked with J. B. Rhine, considered the founder of parapsychology. Her abilities continued late into life. She was in her seventies when Dr. Lawrence Le Shan, a New York psychologist, asked her if she could locate a missing man. After Le Shan gave her a square of cloth from one of the man's shirts, Garrett said that he was in La Jolla, California. Later, it was verified that he'd gone to that city. She also said that he was in his mid-forties, about five feet ten inches tall, and that he'd had a loss in his family when he was between the ages of thirteen and fifteen. Le Shan found out that the man was forty-two, five foot nine, and when he was fourteen his father had deserted the family.

Helpful Hints

Practice regularly. Use different materials—jewelry, cloth, a letter—to see if your psychometry works better for you with a particular material. Also, practice at different times of the day. Try it in the morning, afternoon, and night to see if you have more success at a particular time. By working with different materials and times, you also learn to adapt more easily to various circumstances that might arise when you want to use your skills.

Keep a record of your attempts and successes in your psychic power notebook. Write down the date and time, the place, the object, and your impressions.

Visit secondhand stores and buy a selection of inexpensive trinkets, books, and clothing. See what impressions you get. Who owned the objects, what was their prevailing mood? Some psychics say you should avoid secondhand clothes because of possible unwanted negative influences that you might pick up subconsciously. However, if you're able to consciously detect such feelings, you're much better off. After all, wearing an item of jewelry or clothing from someone who is happy and prosperous might work to your favor.

Exercise: Finding Hidden Objects

Here are a couple of fun ways to practice psychometry with other people. While you can work alone with this talent, it can help to have someone assisting you. Work with a friend or family member who might be interested in psychometry. Make a game of it.

Select a small object that can be easily hidden somewhere in the house. Hold the object as you relax and quiet your mind. Don't try to gain any information from the object. Instead, after you've entered that state of mind where your psychic power works, tell yourself that you are placing a personal detector on the object and that you will easily find it.

Go into a bathroom or closet while your partner hides the object. Make use of the time to reconfirm that you will easily be able to find it. When your partner is ready, confidently begin your search. Imagine that you've just pressed the locator button on the base of your cordless phone to find the missing handset. You hear that beeping and are led right to it. But in this case, instead of the handset, you find the hidden object.

Alternately, you might imagine the hidden object sending out visible pulsations like a blinking flashlight. Whatever your method, know that your personal vibration is attached to the object and you'll be able to find it.

The Making of a Psychometrist

Noreen Renier was involved in publicity and advertising for the Hyatt hotel in Orlando when a psychic asked to make a presentation at the hotel. Renier was a skeptic and didn't want the woman anywhere near the hotel. However, the psychic persisted, and each time Renier was in contact with the woman, her body seemed to vibrate. A short time later, she began to meditate with a friend. During the third session, she felt a sensation like an electrical shock. She began hearing a voice speaking that wasn't hers. When she opened her eyes, her friend was in tears because the voice had delivered a message from her deceased mother.

After that, Renier worked hard to develop her psychic skills. Psychometry seemed a natural talent. At every opportunity, she would touch the rings and watches of those around her and report on the pictures that came into her mind. Her boss didn't appreciate her new interest and fired her. That gave her further impetus to develop her skills and charge for readings. Using her contacts in the hotel industry, she set up shop in a booth at the airport Sheraton in Orlando.

Even from the beginning, Renier took an interest in having her talents validated. Dr. William Roll, the director of the Psychical Research Foundation, tested her skills, and she later worked with Dr. David E. Jones, an archaeologist at the University of Central Florida, who wrote about her talents in *Visions of Time*, a book on his exploration of psychic archaeology.

When Jones met Renier, he handed her a human jawbone, he recalls in his book. She stroked it, frowned, then asked, "Why is he in a hole with a lot of other people?" Renier had no way of knowing, other than through psychometry, that the fossilized mandible was from an adult Native American man who was buried in a mass grave. He died east of the Great Lakes more than two thousand years ago.

When Jones asked what kind of weather the man experienced, she replied, "He didn't like the cold. There was snow. Cold winters and short summers." She said that he was an old Native American man "from up north somewhere."

Jones had worked with other psychics and was trying to verify Renier's abilities. When he asked how the man died, she said he was hit in the head and killed. Jones was impressed. The man's cranium, which was in a separate container in the laboratory, revealed that he had died from a powerful blow to the left side of his head, just as she'd said.

Psychometry at Work

I met Renier in the mid-1990s in the aftermath of her success in locating the body of a missing seventy-six year-old man named Norman Lewis. On March 24, 1994, Lewis, who lived in nearby Williston, Florida, left home in his pickup and vanished. He'd taken nothing with him, not even his wallet. His family hired Renier a year later after police were unable to find him.

Holding a piece of Lewis' clothing, she said that she could see him surrounded by metal and grass, and she could see water. She could see a cliff wall, loose bricks, a railroad track, and a bridge. She also saw the numbers 45 and 21 and said she could see the front of the truck pointed up.

Police Chief Olin Slaughter and Williston Police Investigator Brian Hewitt began putting the pieces together. The area where Lewis disappeared was filled with rock pits and sinkholes. Eventually they concluded that the bridge referred to in Renier's reading was actually an old drive-through truck scale that looked like a bridge. Lewis was found in his truck at the bottom of a water-filled rock pit.

The road to the rock pit was off State Road 45 near railroad tracks. Lewis was found 2.1 miles from his home. The truck was covered by four feet of grass and the front end was pointed up slightly. They found it in eighteen to twenty feet of water below a cliff wall. The case later was featured on an episode of *Unsolved Mysteries*.

Exercise: An Identity Game

Here's an exercise that Noreen Renier uses in her classes on developing psychic skills. It's a good exercise for any teacher to use to get strangers in a new class talking. However, instead of talking about themselves, they'll talk about someone else they don't know! Here's how it works.

Have everyone write down their names and birthdays on a piece of paper, then place the pieces of paper in a bowl. Everyone selects a name, then relaxes and focuses on the name. Then each person gives his or her impressions of the person. Afterwards, ask how many people thought the descriptions fit.

Most practitioners and researchers suggest that anyone can learn psychometry, but some people are naturals. People who work with their hands, who sense things easily through touch, will probably have the most success. The benefits, Renier says, go well beyond the challenge of reading an object: "When you learn these skills, it brings you in touch with your feelings. You're also more in tune with your creative sense. You gain a greater awareness of the people around you as well as a deeper sense of who you are and where you're going. You might also get opportunities to put the skill to practical use to help people in need."

8 Mind Over Matter

It's the most dramatic and wondrous of all psychic powers. It's about using your mind to move objects, bend metal, even levitate objects and create an immunity to fire. It's called psychokinesis or telekinesis, but it's often referred to simply as PK.

Because the effects are so visible and impressive, PK is popular in movies, such as *The Exorcist* and *Poltergeist*, where the power is inevitably out of control or coming from a mysterious or demonic source. Objects hurtle across rooms without being touched. Metals bend like they are made of rubber. The hands of clocks and compasses spin about. People rise from the ground, walk through fire, and are seen in two places at once.

But PK is really about controlling and developing this power that lies within us. Most researchers, in fact, now believe that poltergeist experiences are an uncontrolled psychic ability, often related to an adolescent present in the household, rather than the presence of a nonphysical entity.

Experimental Evidence

The first mind-over-matter experiments go back to the 1930s when a young man walked into the Duke University parapsychology laboratory and told J. B. Rhine that he could influence the fall of dice by the power of his mind. That led to experiments involving dice in which the subject would be told to toss the dice and try to get a particular number to appear. Over the years, many other investigators also attempted the same experiments. Researcher Dean Radin compiled the results of more than one hundred experiments by more than fifty investigators over more than fifty years. He used every experiment he could locate so he wouldn't be accused by skeptics of only selecting the "good" ones. The results showed that a gen-

uine mind-matter effect existed, with odds against chance totaling more than a billion to one.

By the 1980s, investigators were dispensing with dice tossing and instead began using random number generators. Essentially, the subjects were tossing an electronic coin that would come up either as heads or tails. Participants in the experiments were asked to mentally influence the machine so that heads turned up more than tails, or vice versa.

Unlike the wild scenes from movies in which objects are psychically hurled about, influencing random number generators is a tame activity. In fact, there's nothing to see. It's all a matter of statistics. Yet, from a scientific point of view, it is significant when a subject successfully alters the odds of the random numbers produced by the machine.

It would be more interesting, of course, if the subjects were bending metal, such as spoons. However, as Dean Radin explains, scientists like to work with statistics, and random number generators allow for rapid data collection and analysis. Besides, mentally altering the shape of large objects to a noticeable degree apparently doesn't happen very often in laboratory conditions. When it has happened, questions usually arise about how well the laboratory conditions were controlled. But such charges can't be made against random number generators. Because the process is fully automated, there is no way that a subject can contaminate the results.

While the laboratory testing of subjects for PK may seem dry and uninteresting, the stories of some of the practitioners have been anything but dull.

Nina Kulagina

Some of the best-documented psychokinetic exhibitions were those by a Russian housewife named Nina Kulagina who grew up in Leningrad during World War II. By the late 1960s, Nina had developed astonishing psychokinetic abilities that were witnessed by scientists. She would sit at a table and stare at a small object, such as a matchbox or a wineglass, and make it move without touching it. She told investigators that she cleared her mind in order to concentrate on moving her target object. When her concentration was successful, she felt a sharp pain in her spine, and her eyesight blurred.

One of the first scientists to take an interest in her, biologist Edward Naumov, scattered a box of matches on a bench when he first tested her. Kulagina held her hands over them and began shaking as if straining to force the matchstick to move. Suddenly, all the matches moved together to the edge of the bench, then fell one by one to the floor.

Stories of this amazing woman began to reach the West through the international wire services in the spring of 1968. In 1970, William A. McGary, one of a group from the United States investigating psychic phenomena in Russia, described a session in which Kulagina caused several small objects, including a wedding ring and the top of a condiment bottle, to move across a dining-room table. She also caused the wedding ring to rotate on an invisible axis on the table. To make sure that Kulagina wasn't using a concealed magnet or threads, objects were often placed under glass containers and nonmetallic objects were used. Films were also taken of the experiments, which confirm that no known force could explain the movements.

While her abilities were awesome, the experience was physically draining. Kulagina's heartbeat accelerated to 150 to 240 beats per minute, her blood pressure went up, her blood sugar rose, her muscles ached, and she lost up to three pounds in a session.

But not all practitioners of PK think it's necessary to strain or force the objects to move.

Martin Caiden

Martin Caiden, a writer and pilot who wrote more than one hundred science fiction novels as well as nonfiction books on aviation, believed that PK was an ability that anyone could learn with practice. In fact, he had developed his abilities on his own through the use of "energy wheels," miniature windmill-like objects with vanes made of aluminum foil or paper.

I met Caiden in 1988 at a bookstore in Gainesville, Florida, where we were among several writers signing our books at a bookfair event. During the signing, the bald-headed writer, who sported a big, droopy mustache and large glasses, dominated much of the conversation. At times, it seemed that Caiden was holding court rather than participating in a signing. Near the end of the event, he told the other writers about experiments he was conducting that involved psychokinetic energy. He invited, or rather challenged, us to come to his house to see for ourselves. My wife Trish and I were the only ones who took him up on the offer.

That evening, Caiden explained to us that he'd developed psychokinetic power through years of practice, and he had created a special environment for his PK experiments. We went upstairs, where he showed us a large walk-in closet that he'd turned into a laboratory with a window for viewing. A table dominated the room and on it rested at least two dozen light-weight aluminum windmills, each six to eight inches tall. Caiden explained that the room was airtight; the air-conditioning vent was blocked so that no air currents circulated through the room, and the door was surrounded by a rubber seal.

Once you believe it is possible to move beyond the accepted limitations of the human mind, incredible things can happen. Objects can be moved with the mind.

Caiden approached the window and began concentrating. Within a few seconds, two or three of the windmills that he targeted began to slowly revolve. Then others joined and they picked up speed. Some of the vanes rotated clockwise, while others moved counterclockwise. A few of the windmills didn't move at all.

The biggest impediment to success in psychokinetic experiments, Caiden said, is to overcome a natural sense of disbelief. Once you believe it is possible to move beyond the accepted limitations of the human mind, incredible things can happen. Objects can be moved with the mind.

Parapsychologist Loyd Auerbach, who studied Caiden's PK, took up Caiden's challenge and tried to experience psychokinetic power himself. He was successful and described the sensation as almost like an out-of-body experience: "There was a sense of detachment about the experiences while I was having them—almost like I was watching both the objects move (or bend) and watching myself at the same time."

Exercise: Learning PK

You can experiment with psychokinetic power and develop your own abilities. Here's a step-by-step method for learning to move objects with your mind.

1) Begin by simulating psychokinesis through a known force, electrostatic energy. You'll need either a Styrofoam cup or Styrofoam packing material and a wool sweater. Set the Styrofoam on a table in front of you and the sweater on your lap as you sit at the table. Rub your hands briskly over the wool sweater. Then raise a hand or both hands above or to one side of the Styrofoam

object. It should immediately move toward you, either sliding across the table or levitating to your hands.

2) Next, practice with the Styrofoam and wool, but add a mental factor. Focus forcefully on the idea that you can move the object with your mind. You're building your confidence in your ability.

3) Now comes the shift from the use of known energy to psychic power. This time extend your hand without rubbing it against the wool sweater. Focus and imagine a part of yourself merging with the object. See the Styrofoam object moving just as it did before. Firmly believe that you can do it. But avoid straining or striving too hard. Go with it, but don't force it. Just let it happen.

4) Once you're successful moving the Styrofoam without electrostatic forces, go to other lightweight or easily mobile objects, such as a toothpick, paper clip, or pencil. Again, see the object moving and push it with your mind.

Uri Geller

No discussion of mind over matter would be complete without mention of the famous Israeli Uri Geller, who is known as a spoon-bending psychic par excellence by some, and a magician who cleverly fools his audiences into believing that he has genuine psychic power by others. Geller and his chief critic, the magician James Randi, have dominated the public's attention regarding psychic power for more than two decades.

The stories related to Geller's abilities are numerous and virtually impossible to verify. One intriguing incident, reported in 1981, involved teleportation. Supposedly, Geller instantaneously moved from New York City to the suburb of Ossining, where he fell through the roof of a sun porch.

Since Geller was trained as a magician, it's easy to assume that his spoon-bending is a trick, even though he denies it. However, when people in the audience report bent spoons in their possession as Geller bends spoons on stage, the phenomenon becomes even more fascinating. Skeptics, such as Randi, say that the metal was probably bent before the performance but only noticed afterwards. Alternately, the person holding the spoon might've bent it unconsciously while watching the performance, or done it intentionally to trick friends and family members.

I experienced an inadvertent—and somewhat silly—spoon-bending scenario one evening while I was gathering information on synchronicity for this book. When I noticed Geller's name in a book called *Develop Your Psychic Skills*, by Enid Hoffman, I read a paragraph in which the author noted that when Geller performed his spoon-bending feats on BBC television, many viewers found themselves bending metals in their own homes. (Parapsychologists called that experience the PK Induction Effect.) As I was reading the passage, I was eating Tofutti. The nondairy dessert was frozen particularly hard, and when I'd scooped it out of the container, my spoon had bent slightly. I smiled as I looked up from the text to the spoon. Of course my spoon had been bent by known forces. It was a synchronicity, not PK. But as I continued staring at it, the spoon seemed to bend even further on its own.

When I experience something unusual, I always look first to the most likely explanation. In this case, I assumed it was my imagination. After all, I knew the spoon was already bent and I was reading about spoon bending. However, when I went to take another spoonful of Tofutti from the bowl, I found that I now had difficulty scooping it because the spoon was bent too far. In fact, I had to press the bottom of the spoon against my desk to straighten it out in order to continue eating.

Even though Geller remains the most well-known performer of the PK phenomenon, most researchers are mum on his abilities. Richard Broughton wrote several pages about Geller in *Parapsychology: The Controversial Science* and ended by saying, "I trust the reader will forgive me if I decline to take a stand on whether or not Geller's abilities are genuinely paranormal.... Whether or not I believe Geller has psi ability is of little consequence, because all of his demonstrations—even assuming they are genuine—have done little to advance scientific understanding of PK phenomena."

Dean Radin in *The Conscious Universe* takes a tougher stance. He gives Geller only brief mention, simply saying that his performances are outside the realm of science and therefore irrelevant. He gives the same curt dismissal to James Randi and his critiques of Geller.

On the other hand, Bernard Gittelson, author of *Intangible Evidence*, interviewed Geller for his book and came away "convinced of his talent, notwithstanding his penchant for showmanship in a pinch."

I've seen Geller perform on three occasions. In each instance, he was impressive in his telepathic and psychokinetic exhibitions. However, it was impossible to know whether he was tricking the audience or actually using psychic abilities. The last time I saw him, I was hoping he would say that there were two people in the room with the same name. That would've convinced me of his psychic abilities because I was accompanied by a friend who shared the same first and last name with me. Geller, however, didn't come through for us. My impression is that Uri Geller mixes psychic talent with magical effects. It's a complicated scenario that doesn't make for easy answers.

Exercise: Flame PK

Place a lighted candle in front of you. Close off any air currents coming from fans or vents and sit far enough away from the candle so that your breath won't cause the flame to flicker. Make sure the candle is burning directly upright. Sit quietly, stare at the flame, take a few breaths, relax. Now, visualize the flame shooting directly out to the side. Focus your energy on the flame until it bends to your will. Keep in mind that focusing doesn't require straining. Tension in the body can block you from releasing your energy.

Exercise: Water PK

Put enough water in a shallow bowl so that the bowl is two-thirds full. Place the bowl on a table and sit facing it. Focus your attention on the water. Let your mind be calm and clear, then visualize the water swirling in the bowl. See it swirling faster and faster. Create this image in your mind. See it happen. Then, the important final step: Let go of the thought. As you release the thought, you may get the results you were seeking.

Ted Owens

Even more astonishing and controversial than Uri Geller was Ted Owens, known as the PK Man. Owens' extraordinary powers, documented in the 1970s and 1980s by parapsychologist Jeffrey Mishlove and others, supposedly included the ability to produce earthquakes, civil unrest, and strange weather phenomena. He could direct the location and timing of lightning strikes, influence the outcome of athletic competitions, and even cause UFO sightings. Mishlove notes in his book, *The PK Man,* that he delayed its publication for years because he felt that the public was not ready to know about Owens. Owens truly was a wild card in the world of parapsychology, largely because of his claims to be in frequent contact with "space intelligences." Owens' claims were so bizarre that they were often ignored.

One evening in December of 1985, Mishlove received a call from Owens, who sharply warned him that the U.S. government must cancel the next space shuttle flight. "The S.I. (space intelligences) really mean business. They will destroy the shuttle. It's up to you to prevent it," Owens told Mishlove. A month later, on January 28, 1986, Mishlove was "shaken to his bones" when the *Challenger* space shuttle exploded, killing its seven crew members.

Owens' life story is a cautionary tale about psychic power, particularly PK. Owens often acted mentally unstable. He was easily angered, and he vowed retaliation against his critics.

Levitation

Stories of psychokinetic powers, including levitation, go far back into history. A number of Catholic saints supposedly exhibited psychokinetic power. One of the best known is Saint Teresa of Avila, who experienced repeated incidents of levitation that were witnessed by many. One witness, Sister Anne of the Incarnation, in a sworn deposition after Saint Teresa of Avila's death, said:

I was in the choir waiting for the bell to ring when our holy Mother entered and knelt down for perhaps the half of a quarter of an hour. As I was looking on, she was raised about half a yard from the ground without her feet touching it. At this I was terrified and she, for her part, was trembling all over. So I moved to where she was and put my hands under her feet, over which I remained weeping for something like half an hour while the ecstasy lasted. Then suddenly she sank down and rested on her feet and turning her head round to me she asked me who I was and whether I had been there all the while. I said yes, and then she ordered me under obedience to say nothing of what I had seen, and I have in fact said nothing until the present moment.

Here's how Saint Teresa described her experience of being levitated:

It seemed to me, when I tried to make some resistance, as if a great force beneath my feet lifted me up…I confess that it threw me into a great fear, very great indeed at first; for when I saw my body thus lifted up from the earth, how could I help it? Though the spirit draws it upwards after itself, and that with great sweetness, if unresisted, the senses are not lost; at least, I was so much myself as to be able to see that I was being lifted up…I have to say that, when the rapture was over, my body seemed frequently to be buoyant, as if all the weight had departed from it; so much so that now and then I scarcely knew that my feet touched the ground.

Other saints and holy personages of other religions also have reported levitation experiences. Dr. Pamela Rae Heath, an MD who went on to obtain a PhD in parapsychology, notes in her book, *The PK Zone*, that levitation can be faked. However, she writes: "The seemingly universal claims of levitation by religions around the globe—including a few well documented cases in good lighting, outdoors, and with a large number of witnesses—make it seem probable that the phenomenon exists."

Exercise: Levitation

This exercise requires five people, including a subject and four assistants. I remember trying it with friends, and succeeding, when I was a teenager. Recently, I was reminded of it when I witnessed my teenage daughter and her friends duplicate the experiment with virtually the same technique that we'd used many years ago. The longevity of this exercise in human levitation speaks for itself. Something interesting takes place. Here's how it works.

1) The subject sits in a straight-backed chair. The assistants stand on either side of the subject, two to a side. Two of the assistants place an index finger under each of the subject's shoulders, while the other two put an index finger under each knee. Then they try to lift the subject using just the four fingers. Inevitably, they can't do it.

2) Next, the four assistants pile their hands on top of the subject's head as he or she remains in the chair.

3) The group leader, usually the one who encouraged everyone else to try the experiment, now asks the participants to visualize the subject getting lighter and lighter. The leader then addresses the subject: "Imagine that you are lifting up like a helium balloon or a bubble drifting up toward the ceiling. You are as light as a feather. You feel weightless like a ring of smoke. You see yourself floating upwards."

4) The group leader tells everyone to take his or her hands away from the subject's head and again place an index finger below a knee or shoulder. Now the leader tells

participants to lift on the count of the three. This time the subject rises easily up from the chair.

It helps if everyone taking part has an open mind and is willing to believe that it's possible for a group of people to mentally affect matter—in this case, lifting someone with four fingers. While it's not an example of levitation in the same sense as someone lifting up without any help at all, it appears that the four assistants psychokinetically affect the subject, and the subject affects himself or herself in order to help the others accomplish their seemingly impossible task. The success that teens generally experience with this exercise seems to attest to a willingness to withhold judgment and *see what happens*, whereas adults, more set in their beliefs, may find this exercise more challenging.

Exercise: Levitating an Object

You can do this exercise alone or with a group. Place a lightweight object, such as a matchstick, a toothpick, or a small crumbled piece of paper, on a table. Relax and breathe deeply in preparation for your attempt at levitation. Next, focus your attention on the object and sense its weight.

Allow your awareness to become more focused as you mentally feel the object becoming lighter and lighter. Continue breathing deeply and command the object to rise. Imagine it lifting up. See it happening. Keep your attention focused. Try it again and again. You need a strong desire to succeed, a willingness to believe it's possible, and a desire to keep trying when it doesn't work.

The first time you're successful, you may lose your focus, resulting in the object falling back down. However, if you can keep your attention focused, the object might continue to rise.

Exercise: Banishing a Cloud

Here's a PK exercise with atmospherics, one that can have impressive results for anyone within miles to see—if they're looking. Find a small cloud in the sky. Focus on it as you relax and take several deep breaths. Imagine the cloud fading into the surrounding blue sky. You might see yourself painting the sky blue and erasing the little cloud, or you might send a bolt of energy that causes it to vanish. Project a part of yourself outward toward the cloud. Concentrate on the cloud and feel confident that you can wipe it from the sky.

Alternately, select a larger cloud and find a place where you want to cut it in half. Focus on the cloud separating right at that point. For quickest results, you might select an area where the cloud narrows. See yourself slicing the cloud into two pieces. This is a good exercise to do on a long drive, especially if you are a passenger. You can even get the whole family involved in banishing a cloud!

You're probably not going to be able to turn a cloudy day into a clear, sunny one, but if you focus and concentrate you should be able to clear the sky of at least one small cloud. If you show others what you can do, you may encounter someone who says that the cloud probably would have disappeared on its own, or you may wonder yourself if that's the case. To counteract that argument, try bringing a cloud back into existence after you've banished it. Concentrate for the same amount of time that it took you to get rid of the cloud.

Surprisingly, it's not any more difficult to create a cloud than it is to disperse one. Alternately, you can also work with an existing small cloud and focus on making it larger, rather than banishing it.

Fire Immunity

Throughout history certain individuals have exhibited an apparent immunity to fire, demonstrating the power of mind over matter. Fire-walking has been practiced as a spiritual discipline all over the world. In early Greece, priestesses walked barefoot on hot coals in honor of the goddess Artemis. In Italy, devotees of the goddess Feronia walked on glowing pine embers. The Old Testament also refers to fire immunity. Isaiah had a live coal placed on his lips by a seraphim, while Sadrach, Mesach, and Abednego survived unscathed after King Nebuchadnezzar forced them into a blazing furnace so hot it killed the soldiers who led them into it.

At the canonization hearing of Saint Francis of Paolo (1416-1507), eight witnesses testified that they had seen him walk into a fiery furnace to examine the inner damage to it and come out completely unharmed, including his clothes. That was just one of many examples of his fire immunity.

Monks arriving in the New World were surprised to find examples of fire immunity among the Native Americans. The French scribe Friar Lejeune described a fire ceremony near Quebec in which the medicine men picked up red-hot stones and put them between their teeth. The medicine men also rubbed glowing cinders on the bodies of sick people they were attending. Examination showed no burns on either the medicine men or their patients.

Today, fire-walking workshops are widespread and usually emphasize New Age spirituality and positive thinking. After a few hours of preparation, the attendees walk through a bed of hot coals, either wood or mineral. In most cases, the fire-walkers aren't burned by the coals. Skeptics have offered non-psychic, non-spiritual explanations, such as the Leidenfrost effect, the theory that the feet of fire-walkers perspire and trigger a protective seal. Some scientists, though, have dismissed that explanation as nonsense.

There is no trick to fire-walking. You can burn your feet, as some people have found out. As the reality shows on television warn before presenting a dangerous feat: *Don't try this at home.* If you are really interested in fire-walking, I suggest you look for a class conducted by a certified F.I.R.E. instructor. Go to *firewalking.com*, Toby Burkan's Web site. Burkan, founder of the Firewalking Institute for Research and Education, has been leading fire-walking classes since 1977, and is considered the creator of the modern fire-walking movement. His classes have been widely popularized by the motivational speaker Tony Robbins.

Years ago, as a journalist, I had the opportunity to witness an exhibition of a triple immunity—an immunity to fire, to piercing of the skin by broken glass, and to inebriation from a large quantity of alcohol. The incident involved a Cuban *santero*, a practitioner of the Afro-Cuban religion Santeria, which merges Catholic saints and African gods. I met Rueben Delgado at his home in Miami, and we went into a small room outfitted with an altar on which rested statues of saints, a black Madonna, vases of flowers, and burning candles.

He lit a cigar and as he puffed on it, he slipped into a trance and assumed a new personality. In the belief system of Santeria, Rueben had become possessed by a *ser*, or spirit guide. Although Rueben didn't drink alcohol in his normal life, his *ser*, a deceased Cuban slave, drank rum as if it were water. In a matter of minutes, he drank an entire quart. Yet, Rueben

Psychokinetic energy is one of the most controversial psychic powers because of the interaction between mind and matter. It's a powerful ability with enormous potential.

showed no sign of drunkenness. His speech wasn't slurred and he danced gracefully around the room.

Then, to my surprise, he hurled the empty bottle on the tile floor, smashing it into dozens of pieces. Hardly pausing, he continued dancing with bare feet on the broken glass. The soles of his feet should have been badly cut, but there were no jagged wounds, no bleeding. He paused, puffed on the cigar again, then rubbed the glowing tip into his forearm as if it were an ashtray. I was standing right next to him and asked to see his arm. I brushed away the ashes, and even though he gave no indication that he felt any pain, I expected to see signs of a burn, reddened or blistering skin. However, the skin looked perfectly normal.

Psychokinetic energy is one of the most controversial psychic powers because of the interaction between mind and matter. It's a powerful ability with enormous potential. For most people, the challenge of PK is just getting to the point of *believing* that it exists. For others, it's getting a small lightweight object to budge through psychic power. For a few, the challenge is completely different. For those with highly developed talents, mentally moving lightweight objects probably is a minor matter. Like Ted Owens, they might be able to affect the weather, alter events, and influence people's actions. Their challenge is to use their abilities for the greater good, rather than for greed and personal gain.

9 *The Way of Dreams*

*I*n the television series *Medium*, the world of dreams freely interacts with the real world. In fact, Allison DuBois, played by Patricia Arquette, encounters spirits of the dead who help her solve crimes.

Dreams, those mysterious and often baffling movies that play in our sleep, have been on our minds since ancient times. They've been called messages from the gods, a link to the spirit world, a source of great wisdom and guidance, and the royal road to the unconscious. In essence, dreams are an accessible path to psychic power, and the more we learn about dreams—how to evoke them, how to remember them, and how to interpret them—the more we expand our psychic abilities.

Some neurologists (scientists who study the brain) attest that dreams are just a garbled rehash of the day's events. In fact, some dreams are just that, a replay of the day's events, especially if you were involved in any sort of repetitive behavior. For example, if you played computer games for a couple of hours before going to bed, the game might be replayed in your sleep. Those dreams, in which the mind "cools down" from the day's events, are called daily processing dreams. Often, you don't even remember them, or you just recall a snippet.

Another type of dream brings subconscious "junk" to the surface. These so-called psychological dreams make us face something about ourselves that might be blocking us from moving forward. They're often about our fears, anxieties, insecurities, guilt, and resentment. Some of them are nightmares, others are extremely vivid. You could say that they are the "horror" genre of dreaming. Sometimes they are repetitive, like a movie you keep going back to see over and over again. It's probably the subconscious telling you to wake up and listen.

Then there are problem-solving dreams, which are creative in nature and can help us solve a problem or make a decision. Your subconscious—that part of your mind that lies below your conscious awareness—knows all about your problems, and it usually knows how to solve them. If the subconscious or "dreaming self" thinks its solution is important enough, you'll be given a problem-solving dream. You can usually recognize these dreams by the feelings they engender. You might feel a "zing" of recognition, or brief chills or goose bumps. You should be able to link the dream's message to your problem. But even if you don't remember it when you wake up, a similar solution might just pop into your head.

These dreams can be incredibly creative, and they've helped many scientists, inventors, writers, musicians, and others solve problems. Here are some examples of such inventive dreams.

Creative Dreaming

As a teenager, Albert Einstein dreamed he was flying a sled through the sky at faster and faster speeds. When he reached a certain speed, the stars changed shapes and achieved fantastic colors. He never forgot the dream, and thinking about it years later triggered his greatest accomplishment—the theory of relativity. In other words, he literally "dreamed it up."

Mary Shelley's *Frankenstein* was conceived from a dream, and Robert Louis Stevenson dreamed the storyline of *The Strange Case of Jekyll and Hyde* after two days of searching intensely for a plot. "The Nun's Tale" from the *The Canterbury Tales* was inspired by one of Chaucer's dreams. The same was true of Dante's *Divine Comedy*. The famous eighteenth-century composer Giuseppe Tartini was able to complete one of his masterpieces only after remembering one trill from a dream.

Renowned writer Charles Dickens gained the inspiration for many of his characters and plots from his dreams. In interviews with San Francisco radio host Naomi Epel, twenty-six well-known novelists, among them Anne Rice, Stephen King, Sue Grafton, Amy Tan, and William Styron, described how their dreams have influenced their work.

John Robbins got the idea to write his book, *Diet for a New America*, while dreaming. He saw images of animals that talked to him about the relationship between humans and other creatures. The animals advised him to write about the topic. The result was a best-selling book about vegetarianism that was nominated for a Pulitzer Prize.

ESP in Dreams

Then there are the so-called *uncommon dreams*, or those that involve ESP. Although many startling and fascinating instances of ESP have occurred in dreams, don't expect your "everyday" dreams to involve a future event (precognition), mind-to-mind communication (telepathy), or a vision of something actually taking place elsewhere (clairvoyance). There are things you can do to increase your chances of experiencing such dreams, but first, let's take a look at some examples of dreams that feature psychic power.

A Crumbling Foundation

A friend, Bill, told me that he'd dreamed that his family's cabin tilted sideways, as if the foundation was crumbling, and then it collapsed. He knew I'd written a book on dreaming so he asked what I thought it meant. Since most dreams shouldn't be taken literally, I told him to look at the symbol of the crumbling foundation. Was there something in his life that seemed to be falling apart? Unknown to me, Bill and his wife were contemplating a divorce.

But the story doesn't end there. A couple of weeks later he called back and said, "You remember that dream I told you? Well, I was at the cabin over the weekend and guess what. Two concrete blocks on one corner had slipped. The cabin really is in danger of tilting and even slipping off its foundation. We've got people working on it this week." Bill added, almost as an afterthought, that he and his wife had resolved their differences and were getting along better.

So, in this case, the dream could have been both symbolic and a literal message. It was symbolic in that Bill and his wife needed to shore up their differences. As a literal message, it might've been precognitive—a warning of a potential disaster. It could also be seen as a problem-solving dream: Although the deteriorating foundation might not have registered in Bill's conscious mind, his "dreaming self" brought it to his attention.

Lincoln's Dream

In 1865, Abraham Lincoln revealed a startling precognitive dream that has become an unforgettable part of his legend. He told several people that, in the dream, he heard strange sounds of mourning in the East Room of the White House: "Before me was a catafalque on which rested a corpse wrapped in funeral vestments. Around it were stationed soldiers who were acting as guards, and there was a throng of people, some gazing mournfully upon the corpse." Lincoln couldn't see the face so he asked a guard who it was. "The president," the guard in the dream said. A week later, Lincoln was assassinated.

Freud and Jung

The best-known dream analysts were Sigmund Freud (1856-1939) and Carl Jung (1875-1961). Jung was Freud's student but broke away from him when he developed his own theory about dreams. Freud opened the door to the scientific study of dreams with his book *The Interpretation of Dreams* in 1899. Freud believed that neuroses—depression and irrational behavior—were psychological rather than physiological. So he delved into dreams in search of the source of such conditions. He used a technique called free association, which is still used by therapists today.

Freud avoided connecting dreams to psychic abilities; he was mainly concerned with their psychological meaning. He thought that all dreams could be traced to our sexual nature, that repressed infantile wishes and primal urges were disguised in the form of dream images.

Although he is the father of dream research, Freud's perspective on dreams is now widely disputed. In the less inhibited world of today, his ideas seem outdated and particularly biased against women. His perspective is too narrow. But when he called dreams "the royal road to the unconscious," he opened the path to the dream research that would follow.

Jung explored dreams as a path to psychic awareness. Jung believed that, rather than disguising our psychological needs, dreams reveal them. The Swiss-born psychologist thought that dreams expose hidden conflicts or problems and offer hints about the future. He looked for common themes of mythical proportion that spring from the unconscious and appear over and over again in the dreams, folklore, and art of all cultures and all times. He called these universal themes archetypes. According to Jung, these images, like the Hero, the Divine Child, the Wise Old Man/Old Woman, and the Shadow, exist in every culture.

Jung developed his concept of the collective unconscious—a reservoir of knowledge within all of us and the realm of the archetypes—from a dream about entering a basement. In fact, many of his discoveries about the unconscious came to him initially through dreams, his conduit to the deeper mysteries he studied for most of his life. His theories essentially redefined psychology and made it accessible to ordinary people. Jung is probably better known today, more than four decades after his death, than he was at the height of his career as a researcher and therapist.

An Ancient Dream Book

Almost any time you read about dream interpretation, you'll come across something about Jung and Freud. But they were hardly the first dream experts. A man named Artemidorus of Dalis wrote a dream dictionary more than 1,800 years ago. In fact, his book, *Oneirocritica (The Interpretation of Dreams)*, is still in print, a remarkable achievement in itself!

Artemidorus lived in Greece about 140 A.D., and he almost certainly borrowed from older works, such as Assurbanipal's dream book. Assurbanipal, an Assyrian king, lived from 669 to 626 B.C., and his book, written on clay tablets, tells of the importance of dreams for both royalty and commoners. His book was found in the remnants of an ancient library at Nineveh, and it's believed that it was linked to even earlier books, which may have dated all the way back to 5000 B.C.

Artemidorus saw virtually all dreams as prophetic, as did most people of his era. For example, if a slave dreamed of having no teeth, it meant that he would be freed. But Artemidorus also understood dreams as metaphors, which is a common way of approaching dreams today. For example, to dream of kissing someone might be a metaphor for "kiss and make up," or it could mean the "kiss of death," or similarly "kiss it good-bye."

Freud studied Artemidorus' book but wasn't greatly influenced by it. He continued to focus on the idea that dreams are

Your dreams are like your own personal movies that run every night.

related to repressed feelings. Yet, Artemidorus' work has survived and some popular but simplistic dream dictionaries have drawn heavily on his writings. Typically, these dictionaries relate most dream images to good or bad fortune.

Exercise: Recalling Your Dreams

Here one moment, gone the next. Your dreams are like your own personal movies that run every night. Crawl into bed, close your eyes, and wait for the drama to unfold. But what fun is that if you can't remember them in the morning?

Worse yet, some people think that they never dream. But they're wrong. Everyone dreams. Neurologists have proved that. But some people have a hard time remembering even traces of their dreams, so it *seems* to them that they don't dream at all. If you want to improve your dream recall, here's how.

Before you fall asleep, simply tell yourself several times that you'll rest well and remember the most important dream or dreams of the night when you awaken. The best time to make this suggestion is right as you're starting to fall asleep. That's when your mind is most likely to heed your inner command.

If that works, then tell yourself that you'll remember all of your dreams. Often, you'll remember the last one first, and then work backwards. As you recall the second dream, it triggers memories of the one before it.

Imagine you're bringing a dream camera to bed with you. Tell yourself that you'll take dream snapshots during the night, which will be available in the form of memories when you wake up, either during the night or in the morning.

You can also trigger your memory by returning to your favorite position for sleeping. Just relax and ask for your dreams. After a few moments, roll over to the other side. If that doesn't work and you start to drift off again, sit up or stand so that you're forcing yourself to remain awake.

In the morning, try to recall as many details as possible, even if they seem silly or trivial. Don't judge or dismiss any parts that seem extraneous, embarrassing, or negative. Even if you can't remember any dreams at first, ask yourself what you dreamed. Sometimes the request will evoke an image and then another and another.

Recall as many details as you can, then write down the entire dream in a section of your psychic power journal or a separate notebook for dreams. Give the dream a title. Note how the dream felt. Who were the characters? What was your role?

Exercise: Interpreting Dreams

Generic interpretations of dream images, like those found in dream dictionaries, aren't necessarily accurate. You need to translate the images in a way that fits into your life. Here are some guidelines for interpreting your dreams that go beyond the surface interpretations found in such dictionaries. By using these cues, you can delve deeper into your dreams.

- ✪ *Connect dream events with incidents from your waking life.* Keep in mind that such dreams can yield a deeper meaning than simply processing the day's events.
- ✪ *Look for metaphors and puns.* If you dream of a snake slithering through the grass in your direction, you might ask yourself who's the "snake in the grass," the deceitful person in your life. Or, say you dream that someone gives you a spoonful of cough syrup. As a metaphor, "taking your medicine" suggests that you must do what-

ever is necessary to accomplish a goal. Alternately, if you are getting "a taste of your own medicine," you soon may be paying the consequences for something you did. Which one applies to you?

⭐ *Follow your feelings.* How you feel about a dream might be as important as its contents. Note your feelings about the other characters in your dreams as well as the action. For example, does a stranger in a dream make you feel uncomfortable, angry, frightened, happy, or amorous?

⭐ *Monitor your dreaming self.* Pay attention to yourself in your dreams. You're always there, after all, either as one of the characters or as an observer. Some dream researchers even go so far as to say that you are all the characters in your dreams. But usually you have a sense of yourself as the central figure.

Note how you act. Do you flee from challenges or confront them? Do you tend to watch what's going on, or do you jump into the action? Are you older and more mature, or are you younger and smaller? Do you make choices, or do the other characters in your dream make the decisions?

Robert Moss, author of *Conscious Dreaming*, suggests monitoring your dreaming self over several dreams. Seeing how you act will help you interpret the deeper meanings of your dreams and deal with daily problems. Moss writes, "You will find that you will become more observant of the contents of your mind in waking life, and more conscious of how your attitudes shape the reality you think you inhabit."

⭐ *Look for a message.* Your dreaming self may have a message for you, something that you're not willing to face in your waking life. It could be something about your attitude toward yourself or your behavior toward others. Such a message might come to you in a nightmare. Try to take the meaning and turn it into a goal by finding a way to change and improve yourself.

✪ *Watch for warning signs.* It's a good idea to appraise every dream with an eye toward the possibility that it just might relate to something in your future.

For instance, this dream was reported by a seventeen-year-old boy named Jerry, whose parents had recently separated.

I was driving my car through a strange area. A lot of the trees looked black and the ground was blackened like there'd been a forest fire here. I could even smell the burnt wood. Suddenly, my car started shaking. I gripped the steering wheel and then I heard an explosion. The car swerved just like it would do with a blowout. Then I hit something and it flipped over. I crawled out the window. But I was stuck on the side of the road in the burned out forest and it was getting dark. I noticed one green plant poking up through the black landscape and I couldn't take my eyes off it. That's when I woke up in a sweat. I was really relieved that it was a dream.

From a symbolic perspective, the dream image of being stuck on the side of the road suggests that Jerry felt "sidelined." His life was turned upside down. He wasn't able to move ahead. But, in this case, the boy considered the literal meaning of the dream. He took a look at his car and discovered a gash in the left rear tire that could cause a blowout. The dream alerted him to a problem that he wasn't consciously aware of. So, it was also a precognitive dream, and through his alert action, he succeeded in keeping it from coming true.

But in Jerry's case, the symbolic meaning was just as true as the literal meaning of the dream.

While Jerry's dream was personal and unique, some dreams have a familiar ring to many people. That's because they contain common dream themes, such as flying or falling, being unprepared for a test, or losing teeth. For more details on these themes, see pages 177–186.

It is actually possible to incubate or program dreams that will guide you in specific areas of your life.

Exercise: Hunting for Your Dreaming Self

Take a look at the last dream that you recorded and see if you can answer these questions. Keep in mind that your answers will vary from dream to dream. But a pattern related to your behavior in waking life may emerge if you track several dreams.

- ✪ What do you look like? Are you the same as in your waking life? If not, how are you different?
- ✪ Are you present and involved or just observing?
- ✪ Do you take an active role in the action or are you just carried along by events?
- ✪ Do you interact with others or watch them?
- ✪ Are you acting the same as you do during your waking life, or different?

Incubating Dreams

As you get better at remembering, recording, and interpreting your dreams, you can continue to improve and advance your dreaming skills. It is actually possible to incubate or program dreams that will guide you in specific areas of your life. Dream incubation was practiced in ancient times in Mesopotamia, Egypt, Greece, and Rome. People actually traveled to temples dedicated to specific gods, where they spent the night in hopes of receiving a dream that would heal, illuminate, or resolve a problem.

Here's how you can request a dream without leaving your own bed.

Exercise: Cooking Your Dreams

- ✪ The first step in dream incubation is to know when to ask for a dream. The best time to begin your practice is when your desire for an answer to a puzzling question is strongest. Most likely, that's the time when your simmering concern will incubate and bear the fruits of a dream with a message.

- ✪ Formulate a question. Are you concerned about a relationship, a health problem, a career matter, a disruption in your daily life? Make your question simple and direct, but don't ask a yes or no question.

- ✪ Take the practice of dream incubation seriously. Don't ask silly or trivial questions. Keep in mind that the ancients journeyed to the dream temples when a serious matter needed to be resolved.

- ✪ Besides specific questions related to matters at hand, you can also ask broad questions, such as: How can I improve my life? What path should I follow? Why do I feel this way? What am I doing wrong?

- ✪ When you are ready to make your request, imagine that you have entered a dream temple. You might light a candle or turn on some soft music as you prepare your question.

- ✪ Write down your question in your journal before you go to bed. This ritual helps fortify the question in your mind as you go to sleep. Then repeat the question to yourself several times as you start to doze off.

- ✪ Make sure that you are completely open to getting your question answered. Be aware that your dreaming self will provide the truth, even if you don't like the answer.

Awakening
inside a
dream is a
momentous
accomplish-
ment, whether
it happens
spontaneously
or through a
concerted
effort on your
part.

If your dream doesn't seem to answer your question, let it rest. Sometimes, after a few minutes or even an hour or two, the connection suddenly pops into your thoughts in one of those *aha* moments of illumination and understanding. But if you remain stumped, try again. With practice, chances are you will soon begin receiving answers to your questions from your dreaming self.

Lucid Dreaming

Once you're proficient at remembering and interpreting your dreams and even incubating them, you can pursue a higher level of dream work known as lucid dreaming. It's about being consciously aware you are dreaming and able to affect events within the dream. Awakening inside a dream is a momentous accomplishment, whether it happens spontaneously or through a concerted effort on your part. The sensation is extremely exhilarating and memorable, even if the experience only lasts a few seconds. In the lucid state, you can do things that defy normal reality. You can fly, walk through a wall, or dance on the ceiling. The spontaneous and usually joyous experience of dream flying, in fact, might trigger your lucid dreaming experience. Other times, some sensational aspects of the dream landscape might captivate your attention and allow you to become lucid. Or, you might awaken within a dream when you hear powerful, inspiring music, or simply a voice in your ear telling you to look around.

Sleep researcher Stephen LaBerge, who has written two excellent books on lucid dreaming, began his first book with one of his own lucid dreams, in which he finds himself in a magnificent castle. He writes: "As I wandered through a high-vaulted corridor deep within a mighty citadel, I paused to admire the magnificent architecture. Somehow the contemplation of these majestic surroundings stimulated the realization that I was *dreaming*! In the light of my lucid consciousness, the already impressive splendor of the castle appeared even more of a marvel, and with great excitement I began to explore the imaginary reality of my 'castle in the air.'"

To explain his state of mind, LaBerge added, "Fantastic as it may sound, I was in full possession of my waking faculties while dreaming and soundly asleep: I could think as clearly as ever, freely remember details of my waking life, and act deliberately upon conscious reflection."

Creating the Experience

Usually, people experience a lucid dream spontaneously before they attempt to create the experience. If you're not sure whether or not you've had a lucid dream, then you probably haven't. When you do, you'll definitely know it. However, even if you have never found yourself fully awake in a dream, you can still attempt to do so. Intentionally entering a lucid state is not easy, but it's definitely worth the effort.

You might find an opportunity to enter a lucid dream just as you are beginning to fall asleep. As you get drowsy and drift into the first stage of sleep, you'll see a rapid series of "hypnogogic" images flashing in front of your mind's eye. In this state of light sleep, you are still awake. But you must remain so in order to experience a lucid dream.

LaBerge suggests that you first look over your recorded dreams for what he calls "dream signs." That's a term he uses to describe odd dream experiences, which might indicate that you are ready to try lucid dreaming. More specifically, dream signs include:

1) Dream characters, including friends, who transform themselves into other people or other creatures.

2) Strong emotions or intense sensations, such as expanded vision or incredible hearing.

3) Experiencing unusual or impossible abilities, such as walking on water or diving inside the earth.

4) Unusual experiences of time and space, such as finding yourself on another planet or soaring toward the moon. Also, realizing that you dreamed of another time period, the past or future.

I recall one distinctive dream sign: I encountered a twenty-foot-long stalk of celery, then casually carried it home over my shoulder for a salad. If you've recorded some of your dream signs, you're ready to try this method of lucid dreaming.

Exercise: Entering a Lucid Dream

1) When you awaken from a dream, especially early in the morning, think about the details of the dream. Look for dream signs. Go over the dream a few times in your mind. Memorize it.

2) While remaining in bed, spend ten or fifteen minutes writing in your dream journal or reading. If it's still dark, turn on a light so you stay fully awake. If you share a bedroom, you might go into another room.

3) Go back to bed and focus intently on recognizing that you're dreaming.

4) Imagine that you're asleep. See yourself in the dream you just memorized and realize that you are dreaming. Say to yourself: "One, I'm dreaming...two, I'm dreaming..." and on and on. At some point, as you repeat the

phrase, you will be dreaming. As images come to you, look for a dream sign. Then think of something that you might want to do in this dream. For example, maybe you wish to fly or visit a friend.

I came awake in a dream once to find myself in a Southwest desert setting with a small group of people. We were students learning advanced dreaming skills that would allow us to travel into other dimensions. Our teacher was a famous writer and anthropologist. When I questioned him about a comment he made, he became irrationally angry and immediately dismissed me, saying, "You're fired from ninth dimensional kindergarten."

With that, I found myself lying awake in my bed. The dream had been so real that I was confused about how I'd ended up at home and in bed! Had I experienced a lucid dream or was it an out-of-body experience? I wasn't sure. But two months after the experience, the teacher in the dream, Carlos Castaneda, published a real-life book, *The Art of Dreaming*.

In *Conscious Dreaming*, Robert Moss recalls a dream in which he became lucid upon hearing a voice: "A companion I had not previously noticed asked me, 'Where is your body?'—making me aware that I was dreaming and that I was outside my body." Moss' comment shows the close link between lucid dreaming and out-of-body experiences. But there are differences, as you'll see in the next chapter.

10 Out-of-Body Experiences

*I*magine that, as you're going to sleep, you find yourself floating in the air like a hot-air balloon. You look down and see your body on the bed! That's an out-of-body experience, or an OBE. But is it real? Can you really get out of your body? Let's take a look at the evidence and the stories.

One day in the spring of 2004, my daughter came home from high school and told me that one of her friends was going out of body *all the time*. I asked what she meant by all the time. "Like almost every night when she lies on her back," she replied. "She lifts straight up and she can see herself lying on the bed below her."

The fourteen-year-old girl was frightened and disturbed by the repeated out-of-body experiences and so was her mother, who took her to a neurologist. She was given a CAT scan, and to her relief there was no sign of a tumor or other brain disorder. She was told that her "imaginary" experiences were probably related to stress, and she was prescribed a drug to block any further OBEs.

The neurologist thought the experience was related to the functioning of the girl's brain, not her spirit. However, science writer Michael Talbot offers another point of view in his book, *Beyond the Quantum*. He describes an out-of-body experience from his teen years. At first, he thought he was dreaming. But everything in his dream seemed real. Nothing was distorted and nothing about his appearance on the bed below him or the furnishings of his room had changed.

He recalls: "I floated weightlessly out of my bedroom and into the living room, still marveling at the fact that all of the features of the house seemed identical to how I knew them in my waking state....Suddenly, as I swam like some airborne fish through the rooms, I found myself heading on a collision course

with a large picture window. But before I had time to panic, I drifted through it, effortlessly, and looked back in astonishment to see that my passage had not affected it in the least."

He continued drifting along, looking at the dewy grass below him, then suddenly he saw a book in the grass. He moved closer to it and saw that it was a collection of short stories by the nineteenth-century French author Guy de Maupassant. While he was aware of the author, he had no knowledge of the book or any particular interest in it. After that, he lost his awareness and fell into a deep sleep.

The next morning on his way to school, a neighbor girl joined him and said that she'd been walking in the woods near his house and thought she might have lost a library book. She told him it was a collection of short stories by Guy de Maupassant and asked if he'd seen it. "Stunned, I related to her my experience of the night before, and together we strolled to the spot where I had seen the book in the my dream," he writes. "And there it was, nestled in the grass exactly as it had been when I had lazily floated over it."

So what do these experiences mean? Talbot thought his out-of-body experience could have a number of explanations. It could have been a dream that, in a remarkable coincidence, mirrored a real-life incident—the lost book and its exact location.

A second possibility was that information about the lost book had entered his consciousness even though he didn't realize it. Talbot noted numerous studies that show the mind has a remarkable ability to pick up information without our conscious awareness of it. In other words, Talbot might've seen the missing book in his peripheral vision without realizing it. However, he wrote that he had not walked in the area during the time the book was missing, nor had he talked to his neighbor between the times when she lost the book and they recovered it.

The other explanation was that a part of his consciousness left his body during his sleep and he'd actually seen the book. Talbot added that this explanation was the most likely of the three, based on the impact of his own experience as well as cases that he'd read about.

Journeys Out of Body

Journeys Out of Body is the name of a classic book on out-of-body travel by Robert Monroe, a Virginia businessman who recorded his fantastic journeys over three decades. Like most out-of-body experiences, Monroe's experiences occurred spontaneously, and he had no idea what was happening to him. At first, he stopped short of leaving his body.

He would lie down to go to sleep, and within minutes his body would start to shudder violently, and he would feel as if he couldn't move. It took all of his willpower to force himself to sit up and come fully awake. After several such experiences, he thought there was something physically wrong, like epilepsy or a brain tumor. However, his family doctor said he was in perfect health.

At that point, Monroe decided to explore the sensation, which continued to occur over the next few months. One night when the vibrations started up, Monroe realized he could move his fingers. His arm was draped over the side of the bed and his fingers were brushing the rug, so he pressed down with his fingertips. His fingers seemed to penetrate the rug. He pushed harder and his hand sank into the floor.

He returned to his doctor, who advised him to lose some weight, smoke less, and to look into yoga. Some practitioners of yoga, the doctor said, claimed they could travel out of their bodies at will. The very notion struck Monroe as absurd. The vibrations came and went six more times before he mustered the nerve to explore out-of-body travel. Then, one night, with the vibrations in full force, he thought of floating upward—and he did.

The Second Body

That was the beginning of his experiences, which included journeys to the past and future, other dimensions, and even afterlife locales. Monroe became convinced that each of us has a "second body" that takes over when we travel out of body. He learned to initiate OBEs at will and eventually opened the Monroe Institute, where the phenomena is studied and visitors learn how to leave their bodies and embark on their own journeys. They also learn how to objectively gather information in these other dimensional realms, using "maps" and "landmarks" that Monroe charted during his thousands of out-of-body experiences.

How to Get Out

Let's say that you want to get out of your body to see what it's like. Maybe you simply want to hover above your body, conscious and aware, but free of the physical self. Or, maybe you'd like to explore around your neighborhood or even farther, across town, to another city, another country...or even another world! However, you're afraid that you might never find your way back to your body!

That's a natural fear. After all, no one wants to lose his or her body! The good news, though, is that you don't have to worry about it. You can be confident that you always will find your way back. It's as if the part of you that is experiencing an OBE is linked to your sleeping self by an enormous rubber band that snaps you back as soon as you complete your journey.

If you've ever had a spontaneous out-of-body experience, it probably didn't last very long. Usually, the realization that you are out of your body and conscious is overwhelming. You may feel a surge of power, a feeling of incredible euphoria. It's as if you're remembering a piece of your natural heritage that you've forgotten about. Then, seconds later, the fear factor might set in and, instantaneously, you're back in your body.

Getting Protection

Since fear is one of the biggest hindrances to out-of-body travel, it's a good idea to invoke protection before launching an out-of-body journey. At the Monroe Institute, the participants are given the following prayer of protection.

I deeply desire the help and cooperation, the assistance, the understanding of those individuals whose wisdom, development and experience are equal or greater than my own. I ask their guidance and protection from any influence or any source that might provide me with less than my stated desires.

Alternately, you can adapt the way of the shamans, the medicine people of traditional cultures around the world. Their activities involve journeying into the spirit world, and when they do so, they typically invoke a veil of protection.

Hank Wesselman, an anthropologist and author who is also a modern-day shaman, calls on his spirit guides in the "upper world" for protection before he embarks on his journeys. Here's a slightly modified version of the protection prayer that Wesselman uses. Although the language is different from the Monroe Institute's prayer, the sentiments are the same.

I request that my spirit guides provide me with power, protection, and support as I engage in my fieldwork. I also ask that my vibrations be set on high, allowing my traveling second body to journey into the spiritual realms in complete safety, while my physical body awaits my return surrounded by a perimeter of protection. I offer my gratitude and respect in advance.

Invoking protection not only provides an actual safeguard, but it can help you quickly move ahead on your journey. It allows you to drop your fears. It also becomes part of your ritual for entering an OBE. As such, the prayer serves as a trigger. In other words, it signals your body that you're about to embark on another journey. You're safe and ready to go.

Step-by-Step

Whether you've experienced an OBE or not, you can explore the possibilities. Robert Monroe's technique for leaving the body is somewhat complicated, but anyone with a strong will can learn how to do it. First, though, here's a preliminary exercise to prepare yourself.

Why Do You Want an OBE?

Check the answers that apply to you.

- ✪ I want to know what it feels like to get out of my body.
- ✪ I want to fly like a bird.
- ✪ I want to explore other worlds.
- ✪ I want to look in on my friends.
- ✪ I want to prove to myself that the mind can project outside the body.
- ✪ I want to prove that everyone has a second body.
- ✪ I want to visit spirit guides and other nonphysical entities.
- ✪ ....
  (add your own answer).

Using Your Journal

Before you attempt your first OBE using the step-by-step instructions that follow, prepare yourself. In your journal, create a section for out-of-body experiences. First, if you remember any spontaneous OBEs that you've had, write down what you remember and when they occurred, as best as you can recall. Even if you just felt the vibrations or momentarily lifted out of your body, make note of it. You might label these recollections "My Past OBEs."

Next make a list of places that you would like to visit during your OBEs. If you're seeking your first experience, be sure to include modest goals such as hovering in the room. Add a couple of nearby locations, such as other rooms in your house or the area around your house. As you add more potential locations, expand your horizons to a friend's house, to another city, another country. Get fantastic, get totally unreal. Pick some places that you definitely can't reach in your physical body—maybe other worlds, a parallel universe, the distant past, the far future. How about inside a UFO? Be specific.

Once you've got your list, you can also establish goals related to your destinations. For example, an early goal would be to see your body. As you move farther away, you might try to identify specific objects that you can later try to verify. For example, if you visit the backyard of a neighbor's house and see a toy in the yard, you can go look for it the next morning. You also might try to visit a person. See what she's wearing and what she's doing.

Always note a date and time for your attempt, both a beginning time and an ending time. That way if you observe someone, you can ask him the next day what he was doing at a particular time. Keep in mind that you don't have to take your journey at night. In fact, it may help to separate an OBE attempt from your normal bedtime so you won't automatically fall asleep.

Before your first attempt, write down your protection prayer on a separate page of your notebook near the beginning of the section. That way you can easily refer to it. Take a look at the earlier examples and use one, or devise your own. Read it or memorize it and use it before you attempt your journeys.

When the OBE ends, no matter what happened, write down all that you remember. It doesn't matter whether you journeyed to another world where everyone communicates telepathically instead of speaking, or you didn't get launched. It's all part of your journey of exploration.

Exercise: Getting Out of Body

Step 1: Relaxation. Look over the relaxation techniques at the beginning of this book if you're still not familiar with them, or listen to the first exercise on the accompanying CD. Use whatever method feels right to you. The goal is to reach that drowsy state between wakefulness and sleep and to maintain it without falling asleep.

As you become relaxed and start to drift asleep, hold your mental attention on something with your eyes closed. Once you can hold that borderland state indefinitely without falling asleep, you've passed the first stage.

The second stage of relaxation is to maintain the borderland state without concentrating on anything. Just focus on the blackness in front of you. Eliminate any nervousness or unease you might feel.

The third stage involves letting go of your rigid hold on the borderland sleep edge and drifting deeper into consciousness.

That's when the sensory mechanisms should start to shut down. Touch usually goes first, and then smell and taste. Sometimes your vision goes next, sometimes your hearing.

Step 2: Creating the vibrations. This is the critical phase. The vibrational field that is essential to entering an OBE seems easiest to create if your head is positioned in the direction of magnetic north, according to Monroe. Also, make sure your room isn't completely dark; you need some light as a point of reference. In addition, don't set a time limit, and make sure you won't be disturbed.

Without weakening your conscious awareness, relax as deeply as you can, then give yourself the suggestion that you'll recall everything you experience that is beneficial to your physical and mental well-being. Monroe suggests that you repeat this five times, then begin breathing with your mouth half opened.

To set up the vibrational waves, imagine two lines extending from the sides of your head and converging about a foot away in front of your eyes. Think of these lines as charged wires that are joined, or as poles of a magnet that are connected. Once they converge, extend them three feet from your forehead, and then six feet. Now you must move the intersected lines ninety degrees until they are directly over your head. Then reach out toward the point of intersection through the top of your head.

Keep reaching until you feel a reaction. It may feel like a surging, hissing, rhythmically pulsating wave roars into your head; let it sweep through your entire body. At this point, your body may become rigid and immobile.

Step 3: Controlling the vibrations. Once the vibrations start, you need to eliminate the fear and panic that you might experience. The first time you encounter the vibrations, you might feel like you're being electrocuted, even though there is no pain. To escape the vibrations and end the session, simply lie quietly and analyze what's taking place until the vibrations fade away on their own. This usually takes a few minutes.

When you're used to the sensation and have moved beyond any feeling of fear, you're ready to control the vibrations. When the vibrations start, mentally direct them into a ring that sweeps around your body, from head to toes and back again. Once you've got the momentum going, let it proceed on its own. The momentum of the vibrations is critical. The faster the vibrations, the easier it is to disassociate yourself from the physical.

It takes practice to smooth out the vibrations. But eventually, you should be able to start the vibrations simply on a mental command, thus eliminating some of the other steps.

Step 4: Thought control. Now focus on a single thought, such as "float upward" or "up and out." At this point, your thought should instantaneously translate into action. Once again, the fear factor might manifest itself as you begin to rise up from your body. Fear will bring you immediately back to your familiar place of residence—your body.

Step 5: Separation and lifting out. On your first attempt, you might just separate your hand and explore the area immediately around you. Find an object, maybe something on a bed stand. See if you can identify it by touch.

Once you're comfortable with this partial disassociation, the easiest way to fully separate from your body is to imagine yourself lifting out and floating upward. Think about how pleasurable the sensation will be. Feel yourself getting lighter and lighter. If you maintain these thoughts, you'll float up and out. You can also rotate your way out, as if you're slowly turning over in bed.

When you're out, you can explore your immediate area. If you want to go farther, simply think about where you want to go. The clearer your request, the faster you move ahead toward your target.

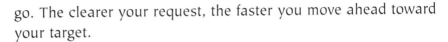

Summary

Briefly, the steps to entering an OBE are as follows:

1) You relax deeply without falling asleep.

2) Next you set up the vibrational waves.

3) Then you smooth them out.

4) You suggest to yourself that you will float upward, then imagine yourself lifting up and out.

What does it feel like to get out? Usually, it's a sense of great exhilaration. But it varies from one person to another. Here's how Girolomo Cardano, a sixteenth-century mathematician, physician, and astrologer, described his experiences: "When I go into trance I have near my heart a feeling as though the spirit detached itself from the body, and this separation extends to all the body, especially the head and neck. After that, I have no longer the idea of any sensation, except of feeling myself outside my body."

Once you've succeeded, you should be able to create the vibrations with relative ease. At that point, you can explore not only this world, but other worlds, including the realms of spirit. What you do with those experiences and how they affect your life will be up to you.

Inevitably, when you experience an OBE or a lucid dream, you'll come to accept that you are more than your physical body and you can perceive far more than the physical world. With practice you'll recognize that, at your core, you are a spiritual being temporarily inhabiting a physical body.

★ ★ ★

With practice you'll recognize that, at your core, you are a spiritual being temporarily inhabiting a physical body.

★ ★ ★

11 Spirit Contact

*T*hey're called ghosts, spirits, or apparitions. Although they're renowned for frightening mortals, the so-called spooks are far fewer than you might imagine. Most anecdotes about ghostly encounters either feature benevolent spirits or apparitions who pose no threat.

In the movie *Ghost*, the bond of love between the two main characters is so strong that when Patrick Swayze, who plays the male love interest, dies, he's incapable of letting go. He haunts his lover, played by Demi Moore, who senses him but can't see him. He eventually finds a medium, played by Whoopi Goldberg, who can see him, and convinces her to pass on an important message to his lost love.

Often a dying person, or one recently deceased, contacts a loved one. Sometimes, as in the following case, the contact is made with a stranger. Dr. Christiaan Bernard, the South African surgeon who became world renowned after he performed the first heart transplant, related this tale during an appearance on Italian television. The mysterious incident took place eighteen years earlier on a night when he was resting in a private hospital room.

Bernard recalled: "My bed was near the window and there was some light coming from outside. Around 10 P.M., a woman entered the room. She walked toward my bed, put her hand on my chest, and began pushing against it. I looked up at her and saw she was very thin and pale, with blue eyes and gray hair. She was pressing strongly on my chest. I took her wrists in my hand. They were very fragile. I pushed her back and realized that she was extremely light. Then, as if she were reacting to my pressure, she levitated and disappeared through the window."

Bernard rang for a nurse, but several minutes passed before one appeared. The nurse apologized, saying she couldn't come

right away because a woman was dying in her ward right at the time he buzzed. "I asked her to describe the woman," Bernard said. "She told me she was thin with blue eyes and gray hair, and was wearing a white nightgown—the same woman I'd seen!"

While Bernard's account is peculiar in that he didn't know the woman and that he experienced physical contact with her, stories of appearances by deceased loved ones abound. In the aftermath of my father's death, my mother often sensed his presence. While it's not surprising that someone suddenly alone would think about a lost spouse, my mother felt there was something more involved. One frigid winter day, the letters M-A-C were spelled out on a frosty window near the chair where my father often sat and read books. Mac was the nickname he went by. On another occasion, my mother saw a glowing ball of light across the room from her. She watched it for several seconds before it vanished. She was sure it was a spirit image of her husband of more than fifty years. She found these manifestations comforting. A few years after my father's death, my mother met a man who'd lost his wife and they began seeing each other on a regular basis. Apparently satisfied that she was being well taken care of, my father made no further appearances.

The contact my mother described to me is hardly unusual. In fact, psychic Ingo Swann wrote: "The appearance of the spirit of a departed loved one is so common it's a wonder it's controversial."

What Is a Ghost?

Is there a difference between a ghost and a spirit? The distinction can be difficult to discern. Both are capable of physical

manifestations. When a spirit, especially a recently deceased loved one, makes contact, it's probably to pass a message of love or create awareness that life continues. Some spirits are said to make regular visits to help out people in need, but they're also fully aware of their existence in the spirit world.

A ghost, on the other hand, is confused and lost, clinging to the earth plane, possibly unaware that he or she has died. Often, there is a strong emotional or material tie that makes it difficult for the deceased individual to move on. In other words, the ghost is stuck between this world and the other side.

Ghosts tend to follow a regular routine, and hauntings are often predictable. The ghost might walk down the same corridor, stop at the same place, and disappear in the same manner. The sounds of footsteps, creaking floorboards, and doors opening and closing might follow the same pattern with each appearance. Some of these apparitions might be residual hauntings, which are energy patterns imprinted at a location where strong emotions have been experienced. In such cases, there is no conscious entity involved.

A ghost is usually a stranger and is often associated with a particular place where he or she lived or died. Old hotels, theaters, graveyards, and historical buildings often are said to be haunted. But ghosts have been reported in many other places that normally wouldn't be thought of as haunted. Among them are busy restaurants, airplanes en route from one city to the next, even a section of highway built over an Indian village.

Science and Ghosts

Although parapsychologists have been interested in ghosts as well as telepathy, precognition, and other psychic powers, laboratory research is virtually nonexistent. As one parapsychologist put it, "No respectable ghosts would manifest in a laboratory, especially not upon command." However, when the laboratory equipment is moved to haunted sites, ghosts have not only come out, but their appearances have registered on electronic equipment.

Ghost researchers use electromagnetic field meters, like the TriField Natural EM Meter, because changes in electric fields have long been associated with hauntings. Meters measuring radio waves, cameras with infrared film, tape recorders, and temperature measurement devices are also part of the investigators' arsenal.

When the Shelbyville, Kentucky, police department moved its headquarters into a partially restored building erected in the 1920s, the officers soon heard footsteps on the stairs at night when no one was there. Doorknobs turned, desk drawers opened on their own, and strange hot zones formed in air-conditioned rooms. Finally, in the fall of 2003, after months of odd experiences, the police called for outside help. They contacted the Scientific Investigative Ghost Hunting Team (SIGHT) in Louisville.

The investigators approached their target, as they always do, from a negative point of view. In other words, they wanted to prove that the mysterious sounds and movements were created through normal means. Steve Conley of SIGHT says that nine out of ten times, they find natural explanations. However, by the fall of 2004, a year after the investigation was initiated, the case remained open. No definitive source of the strange phenomena had been found.

Ghost Photography

Photography is probably the most controversial, as well as the oldest, mechanical tool used in ghost hunting. Photos of transparent figures date back to the late nineteenth century, and many of them are now considered fraudulent. Much more common than images of human figures are orbs of light floating or hovering in photos taken at haunted locations. Researchers consider some of these photos to be convincing, but many are not.

The realm of ghost photography remains plagued by technical problems that raise many doubts. Besides outright fraud, bad film, overlapping pictures, flash reflections, and long exposures, there are a few other possible explanations of ghost photos. Some have been faked intentionally, others accidentally. "Ghost" images can be created simply by cigarette smoke, a camera strap hanging in the field of view, reflections off a shiny surface, or a finger in front of a lens.

In recent years, digital cameras have been used because they function well in low light. But the orbs that appear in some photos taken during ghost-hunting sessions are often digital flaws. A speck of dust on the lens or a reflection off a shiny object can produce the same image.

While ghost hunters use an array of electronic equipment in their investigations, many of them also use psychics. They've found that some people have the ability to detect ghostly entities and even come up with verifiable information on deceased former residents who might be responsible for the haunting.

If you're interested in pursuing ghosts with your psychic power, here are several steps to follow.

Ghost Hunting

⭐ If you know of a haunted residence and have access to it, you're on your way. Or look for public buildings in your area that have a history of hauntings. Otherwise, consider visiting a graveyard, especially an historic one such as the graveyard at Gettysburg where Confederate soldiers are buried. That burial ground is known as a haunted site.

✪ Consider joining a ghost-hunting group in your area. The Internet lists dozens of such organizations. Contact someone in the group by phone or e-mail. Find out if they use psychics in their investigations. If so, say that you would like to work with a psychic on a case to help develop your skills.

✪ Once you've selected your site, make arrangements for a visit and arrive with a positive attitude that you'll make the contact you're seeking. If you're going to a graveyard or public building, follow all the related rules and laws. Ask permission to enter any private areas. Don't trespass on either a public building or private residence.

✪ Find a place where you can sit quietly and calm your mind as you focus on your breath and enter your psychic space.

✪ Request protection from a higher spiritual entity or spirit guide against any adverse reaction if contact with a ghost is made.

✪ Move about the area or room where the ghost has been sighted and try to sense the entity. You may feel a chill in the air; hear inexplicable sounds, such as a creaking door or footsteps when no one else is present; smell an aroma, such as perfume or tobacco; see flickering lights; or glimpse a manifestation, either in human form or as a globe of light.

✪ Remain calm and ask the entity why it is here. If you get a response, ask follow-up questions, such as the identity and background of the ghost.

✪ Offer a blessing to the entity, and if it feels appropriate, tell the ghost that it's now time to move on.

✪ As soon as possible, write down in your journal or notebook details of what happened. Note the date, time, location, and also the names of others present. Record all the sensations you experienced and any messages.

Cassadaga

You may feel odd attempting to contact the spirit world. But you're not alone in your endeavor. There's a town in central Florida where virtually all the residents communicate with spirits on a regular basis.

When you enter Cassadaga, you step into the world of spiritualism, of mediums. Rather than a town or village, it's called a spiritualist camp, and it's located in a hilly pine forest forty minutes from Disney World. For thousands of people who journey there each year, Cassadaga is a crossroads for the spirit world. Spiritualists, as the name suggests, believe a thin veil exists between our world and the spirit realm, and that veil can be penetrated by mediums.

Cassadaga was founded in 1876 by spiritualist George Colby, who was led to the village site in the forested Florida interior by Seneca, his Native American spirit guide. Colby and his friend, T. D. Giddings, built houses on the shore of what is now known as Lake Colby. Colby obtained a government deed for seventy-four acres for the community, but eighteen years passed before the community was established. In October 1894, twelve mediums signed the charter for the Cassadaga Spiritualist Camp.

Since then the village has alternately flourished and floundered. The popularity of spiritualism in the early twentieth century attracted crowds and séances that included physical manifestation of spirits, spirit rapping, aports (materialization of objects) and ectoplasm (etheric matter from the spirit world), and exhibitions of levitation. Visitors stayed at the village's Mediterranean-style hotel built in the 1920s. But accusations of fraud were rampant, and eventually spiritualism's popularity faded. With the interest in New Age belief, the community has experienced several revivals since the late 1960s. The hotel has been renovated and its rooms fill up on weekends, especially in the winter, which is known as "the season."

I've visited Cassadaga on several occasions and received readings from the mediums in the village. Some of the readers made predictions that came to pass. Others were not as accurate. But one particular reading stands out. The medium, Hazel Burley, told me something that would make sense only to me. She said that someone with the letter J was coming through to her. She put her hands to her head and said that his death had related to the brain. Then she frowned and said, "There are more than one."

That sounds confusing, but it wasn't to me. That's because I knew two men, Jay and John, who had died in the previous year of brain cancer. One was a longtime friend, the other a cousin. The main point of the reading seemed to be recognition of their presence rather than any particular message.

But was Hazel obtaining the information from the spirits of Jay and John, or was she picking it up telepathically? In my case, I hadn't been thinking of either one of the J's prior to the reading and had no intention of seeking out either one. Yet, the question of telepathy always lingers around mediumistic contact with the dead.

As with many aspects of psychic power, direct experience creates personal proof, and I'd had such experiences with both men near the time of their deaths. John had appeared to me in a dream. He was smiling and looked happy. But he seemed somewhat confused. He asked me what was going on. My sis-

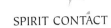

ter was also in the dream. At the time, I knew my cousin was dying of brain cancer. Two days later, my sister called to tell me that she'd just heard that John had died.

I also dreamed about Jay a few months after his death. His appearance was somewhat baffling because he and a companion-guide were dressed in ski jackets in Florida. After a gathering of friends and relatives, the pair skied off down a mountain slope, the guide close by Jay's side. Fascinated by the appearance of the mountain, I ran down the slope and soon discovered it wasn't an ordinary mountain, but a passage between worlds or dimensions.

A Resident Ghost

On my first trip to Cassadaga I didn't have to leave the Cassadaga Hotel to experience a ghostly encounter. It was a quiet weekday at the camp in the mid-1980s, and part of the hotel was closed for renovations. As a result, my wife and I were the only occupants. It was a memorable night. It was close to 1 A.M. and we were awake reading when we heard the sound of heavy footsteps stomping down the hallway toward our room. It sounded as if someone wearing heavy lead-soled boots was intentionally disrupting the quiet.

We both hurried toward the door. I was about to open it to take a look when I felt a cold chill and a ball of dread in the center of my body. Trish felt the same way. My hand wouldn't work. I couldn't open the door. The loud, terrible stomping continued. At that point, we did something that we later laughed about. We shoved the dresser in front of the door. We didn't want whatever was out there to get into the room. We were that frightened. We kept the dresser there until morning.

Later we learned that the hotel was haunted. Considering its location, we should have figured as much.

Another Ghostly Encounter

During the summer of 2004, we experienced another ghostly encounter at a beachfront hotel in the town of Cabarette in the Dominican Republic. Our hotel, oddly enough, was located adjacent to a graveyard. Our one-bedroom condo featured an ocean view—that is, if we gazed beyond the gravestones scattered on the dunes. The closest graves, in fact, were less than one hundred feet from our room.

On our second day at the hotel, we found the gate to the graveyard open and walked inside. We thought we would find ancient graves, but that wasn't the case. Two of the first three gravestones we examined listed a date of death within the last several months. Something about a fresh grave is more disturbing than an ancient one. We were about to leave when we saw a man walking toward us. He was a gravedigger and had just uncovered a coffin as he was digging a grave in the far corner of the graveyard. He explained that below the graveyard was another one that had disappeared years ago under the rising sand. When he invited us to take a look, we thanked him for his hospitality and said we had to leave.

Later, we asked the owner of the hotel about the graveyard, and he assured us the spirits were *muy tranquilo*—very calm— and brought good energy to the area. "It's not like the movies," he added with a smile. However, on our last night at the hotel, we were given an unusual sendoff that seemed to emanate from the other side.

Three Knocks

We went to bed early, around ten or ten-thirty. I woke up at about eleven when I heard voices in the adjacent room. I walked out and was puzzled to find the television on, since we hadn't watched it all evening. I turned it off and went back to bed.

I soon fell asleep again, but was awakened between 11:15 and 11:30 by the sound of heavy pounding at the front of the building. It was rhythmic. Two loud, hollow thumps, then a third thunderous strike that sounded like a wrecking ball hitting the building. The pattern was repeated again and again. Each time, the third strike was felt so powerful that the building and the bed shuddered. There was also an eerie energetic resonance to the pounding, almost as if it were happening in a dream instead of real life.

I listened to the pattern for a couple of minutes trying to figure out what it was. Finally, Trish turned over and I asked her if she heard it. She said she did and that it woke her up, even though she is deaf in one ear and sleeps on her good ear. We both wondered what it was and simultaneously sat up. At that instant, the pounding stopped. There was no sign of any activity outside the building. Unlike the experience in Cassadaga, I never felt frightened. I was actually left with a feeling of wonder.

The next day we reported the noise to the owner and his wife, who both looked confused and wary. The wife said she heard that a telephone pole had fallen down about a kilometer away, possibly from a minor earthquake. But earthquakes aren't rhythmic, and when we checked an earthquake site on the Internet, none was reported in the Dominican Republic that night.

But there was that graveyard. Were the spirits calling out to us, as if to raise our awareness, or say farewell? Had we been selected because we entered the graveyard and expressed our curiosity? We'll probably never know, but we both left the hotel with a feeling that we'd made contact with the other side.

Later, we learned that many others have reported a mysterious phenomenon known as the "three knocks of death." These uncanny incidents have been reported all over the world. Here's one such incident.

In 1979, a Mrs. Hughes of Everton, England, heard three loud raps on her front door. She was standing near the door and opened it within a few seconds. There was no one there, which didn't really surprise her, since she hadn't heard the sound of her squeaky front gate being opened, which always warned her of impending visitors. She closed the door feeling slightly perplexed and glanced at the clock, noting that the time was exactly 11 P.M.

Half an hour later, there was another knock, and this time Mrs. Hughes was confronted by two policemen who gave her the tragic news that her husband, Bobby, had been killed that evening. Two years later, Mrs. Hughes was watching the news when she and her daughter both heard three loud raps on the kitchen window. When they stepped outside, no one was there. Fifteen minutes later, Mrs. Hughes opened the front door and was horrified to find the body of her brother lying dead on the front step. He'd died of a heart attack.

Spirit guides are unseen helpers who might whisper a suggestion or nudge you in the right direction at the right time.

What's a Spirit Guide?

Spirit guides are unseen helpers who might whisper a suggestion or nudge you in the right direction at the right time. Like ghosts, spirit guides are controversial. Some scientists dismiss them as wishful thinking. Others suggests that spirit guides are part of our unconscious. A common New Age belief is that guides are separate entities who have died, crossed over, and then come back to assist us on the earth plane. These beings are aware of their state as well as their role as guides.

Enid Hoffman, author of *Develop Your Psychic Skills*, says that guides come and go with our needs: "Each guide is assigned to teach a particular lesson. When you are finished, that guide leaves and a new one comes."

Hoffman also says that guides don't direct your life and won't interfere unless you're headed toward self-destruction. Guides may be departed family members or entities that you've never met, at least not in the physical world. They're available when you need them, just like a friend you might call.

While those who look for ghosts may be seeking proof of existence beyond this life, those who seek to contact spirit guides are usually looking for advice and information. One way of contacting a spirit guide is to go to a medium as I did in Cassadaga. But you can also use your psychic power to seek out a guide on your own. Here's how.

Exercise: Contacting a Spirit Guide

⭐ Think of a question you want answered. Write it down to reaffirm the question. Make sure that your question is serious rather than trivial, and specific rather than overly general. Also, don't ask a simple yes-no question. Phrase it so that you're requesting an explanation or information.

⭐ As always when you are turning inward, take time to breathe deeply and relax.

⭐ Request that the entity or entities that you contact from the spirit world will have your best interest at heart. You might visualize a veil of white light surrounding your body and protecting you.

⭐ Quiet your mind. You might imagine emptying a pitcher as you release all the internal chatter. Focus on your question.

⭐ Imagine yourself in a beautiful place in nature. Possibly you're walking along a trail through a forest. You can smell the rich scents of the forest and earth. You feel the pine needles beneath your feet and hear the call of birds. Shafts of sunlight filter through the trees. You come to a creek and follow it, listening to the water flowing over the rocks. You find an opening in the forest near the creek and settle into a place that feels right for you. Relax and enjoy the serene setting. Then, as you look into the distance along the creek, you see a distinct globe of light. It grows larger and brighter as it moves toward you, and then it takes on human form.

✪ Notice how comfortable you feel in the presence of this being who has joined you. Find out your guide's name. Ask whatever question is on your mind and discuss any problems.

✪ When your conversation is complete, thank your guide for the assistance and ask if you can meet again at this same place. Walk away from the clearing and return from your journey.

✪ If you don't make contact with a spirit guide, it could mean that you're not yet ready for the encounter.

When I attempted this exercise as I began writing this chapter, I asked my spirit guides for assistance. The response I received came in a brief, terse message: *Do your research.* When I contacted my guide again after writing the draft of this chapter, I asked for a message for my readers regarding the spirit world. Here is what I was told: *There are groups of spirits working together for common goals. We are bonded by beliefs and intentions. Some of us work with people in your world. Our goals vary depending on our common interests. The ultimate goal is ecstasy.*

12 The Future of Psychic Power

*L*et's say that you accept psychic power. You've read about the studies, the evidence, the laboratory experiments, and all the anecdotes told by people who have experienced it. Let's say you've even experienced it yourself. So it's real, right?

Dean Radin thinks so. "The reality of psychic phenomena is no longer based solely upon faith, or wishful thinking, or absorbing anecdotes," he writes in *The Conscious Universe*. "It is not even based upon the results of a few scientific experiments. Instead, we know that these phenomena exist because of new ways of evaluating massive amounts of scientific evidence collected over a century by scores of researchers...The fact is that virtually all scientists who have studied the evidence, *including the hard nosed skeptics*, now agree that something interesting is going on that merits serious scientific attention."

But hold on. In spite of all the supporting evidence, some scientists and journalists continue their efforts to discredit all psychic abilities. The dominant thinking of our society, perpetrated by mainstream science, says that psychic power is impossible, that such abilities, if they were true, would violate the laws of nature.

But which natural laws would be violated by psychic power? The critics never say because, as Radin points out, "The assertion is groundless—the laws of nature are not fixed absolutes. They are fairly stable ideas that are always subject to expansion and refinement based on evidence from new observations."

The reason some people disregard psychic power has less to do with science than with belief. We tend to perceive the world not as it is, but as we wish it to be. Someday, however, those who reject the evidence may be compared to the hardcore skeptics who refuse to believe that man has walked on the moon. In spite of all the evidence—the photos, the historical

data, the moon rocks, and the testimonials of those who went to the moon and returned—they are convinced it never happened. Of course, they are out of the mainstream.

In a sense, we've already gone to the moon with the investigation of psychic power. We've got the experimental evidence. Maybe all that is lacking are the "moon rocks" of psychic power—the ultimate evidence that will trigger a shift to the side of psychic phenomena.

So where are these psychic moon rocks? They're within each of us. Ultimately, the external evidence only counts so much. The moon rocks, in this case, are our personal experiences of the power within us that extend beyond perceived mental limitations.

In some respects, it seems that an evolutionary shift in our mentality is so far off that it's out of sight. After all, radical religious fundamentalism seems to be on the rise around the world, including the United States. Scientists for the most part are entrenched in the old paradigm in spite of developments in quantum physics that call that framework into question. Psychic power is associated with fraud and deception, and there are plenty of charlatans motivated by greed and power to support that belief. Meanwhile, the U.S. government opposes the use of remote viewing to fight terrorism because politicians know that their opponents will attack them if they endorse the use of psychics. As former CIA remote viewer Joe McMoneagle puts it, "Killing people with napalm is not viewed as negatively as using psychics to hunt terrorists—go figure."

Yet, in spite of opposition and negative sentiments, we could be closer to a shift in consciousness than you might think. Scientists say that evolutionary change is not necessarily a slow process; in fact, it appears to happen all at once. If the root of evolution is consciousness, as some scientists think, an evolutionary shift in consciousness could happen at any time.

Although mainstream acceptance of psychic power may seem less than an evolutionary step in human development, the results could be extraordinary. When these abilities are accepted, developed, and practiced, the world will change. Space travel would be instantaneous, without the need for rocket propulsion. History would be studied first-hand by remote-viewing historians. Medical treatment would leap ahead as doctors could literally travel into the patient's body to diagnose and heal. The possibilities are endless.

The old world would end, a new world would begin. But that won't happen until we overcome our fears and no longer need to use our advancements to conquer, control, and manipulate. When enough people encounter their true inner natures and realize the physical world is a manifestation of consciousness, and not the other way around—that we are truly spiritual beings experiencing a physical existence—then a shift will occur and we will move into the next phase of human development.

Common Dream Themes

*I*t's one of the mysteries of the dream world. Why do so many people dream of flying or falling, being unprepared for a test, losing teeth, or finding themselves nude in public? These are just a few of what's known as common dream themes. Common, in this case, means familiar, not ordinary.

What follows is a list of some of the most common dream themes along with more details. How many of them strike a chord with you?

These dreams, generally speaking, may represent recurring problems that many of us experience. Sometimes, the dream is repeated over and over as our unconscious minds or dreaming selves hammer the message home. Keep in mind that dreams are individual, and the meanings may vary from person to person. Take into consideration all the elements of your dream—the characters, the events, and how you feel about the dream—as well as the dream theme.

- ✪ Flying dreams
- ✪ Falling dreams
- ✪ Travel dreams
- ✪ Losing keys, billfold, or luggage
- ✪ Attending school and taking tests
- ✪ Being nude
- ✪ Teeth falling out
- ✪ Finding money
- ✪ Water dreams
- ✪ Finding a bathroom
- ✪ Death dreams

Flying Dreams

It's one of the most delightful sensations you can experience in a dream. The act of soaring away with a sense of lightness and control is extremely exhilarating, a sensation to be savored

and remembered. You can fly around inside your house, around the neighborhood, or to the stars.

Although Sigmund Freud thought flying dreams related to a driving desire for a close relationship, most therapists today favor Carl Jung's explanation that such dreams are related to a sense of breaking free of restrictions. It's an uplifting experience (pun intended). In fact, you might be rising above your problems. Such dreams usually relate to positive changes in your waking life.

Here are some questions to ask yourself about your flying dream:

- ✪ How did you feel while you were flying?
- ✪ Are you fleeing something or someone, or are you simply enjoying yourself?
- ✪ Do you have any trouble taking off or holding your altitude?
- ✪ Does this dream seem familiar as if you've experienced it before?
- ✪ Do you feel in control of your flight?
- ✪ Can you relate the feeling of flying to anything happening in your waking life?

Falling Dreams

Falling dreams can be scary, but no one ever dies in this type of dream. You can hit the ground and live to tell about it. These dreams can come in many different forms—sometimes you're pushed, other times you trip. You might fall off a building or a mountain, or from an airplane.

A falling dream may contain an important message telling you to watch your step. Or it might suggest that you're moving in the wrong direction, possibly on a dangerous path. Such a dream could also be a metaphor for a fall from grace or falling on hard times:

Here are some questions to consider about your dream of falling:

✪ Do you know why you're falling?

✪ How do you feel about the fall?

✪ What caused you to fall in the dream?

✪ What event or events led up to your fall?

✪ Is there anything in your life that reminds you of the fall and the incidents leading up to it?

Travel Dreams

The important thing about dreams of mass transportation—trains, planes, and buses—is what you are doing there and what's going on. Are you waiting in the station? Are you worried about missing a plane? Have you lost your ticket? Are you feeling lost and confused by all the train lines in the station? Or, are you traveling rapidly and feeling the thrill of the speed?

Dreams of travel can often reflect the difficult changes you are going through in your life. If you're dealing with uncertainty, you might find that you have such dreams more frequently. You might misplace your ticket or worry about catching the plane, train, or bus on time.

As a metaphor, taking trains might indicate that you're "in training." Likewise, waiting in a train or a bus station might relate to concerns about not moving ahead; in other words, being stationary. Travel dreams might also represent the journey of your life.

Here are some questions to consider about your dream of traveling:

✪ What's the most important thing you're doing in your travel dream?

✪ How do you feel about it?

✪ Are you traveling with anyone?

✪ Do you know where you're going?

✪ If you're having difficulties on your journey, do you know what's causing it?

✪ Does the dream remind you of something going on in your waking life?

Losing Keys, Wallet, Purse, Luggage

These things usually relate to security and identity. These disturbing incidents sometimes take place within a travel dream. So losing valuables like keys, a wallet, a purse, luggage, or other valuables might indicate a worry about your security, your loss of identity, your sense of belonging, or your self-worth.

Such dreams probably make you feel uncomfortable. It's your inner self's way of getting you to confront your fear or concern about losing sense of who you are, what's important to you, and possibly where you are going.

To find out what your dream of losing something of value means, ask yourself these questions:

✪ What does the lost object mean to you? What is its purpose?
✪ Is it related to your identity or to something you possess?
✪ How did you feel in the dream about losing the object?
✪ Is there anything going on in your life in which you feel the same way?

Taking a Test

Taking tests is a common dream theme, even among adults who haven't been in a school setting for many years. In these dreams, you're usually unprepared for the test. It might be a classroom test, or you might realize you have to give a speech or go on stage to perform. Whatever it is, you're not ready. You haven't studied; you haven't done your homework. You're afraid of failing or making a fool of yourself.

Sound familiar? Unlike some of the other dream themes, the dream of taking a test can have a very literal interpretation. You actually may be concerned about being unprepared for a test, a speech, or a performance. Many adults call this dream, the "college dream," because they find themselves back in college and unprepared for a test. They might also realize that they haven't even attended classes. Such a dream might occur if the person is concerned about being qualified for some new challenge in his or her life, such as a new job, or an advancement in the present one.

If you've had a dream about a test that you were unprepared to take, ask yourself these questions:

- ✪ Is there a test coming up that you've forgotten about?
- ✪ If not, what significant event is taking place in your life?
- ✪ Are you being tested in relation to the event?
- ✪ How prepared are you to deal with it?
- ✪ What lessons can you learn from the dream?
- ✪ How can you be better prepared?

Being Nude

While dreams about being unprepared for a test might have a literal meaning, you don't have to worry about that if you dream of being naked in public. These dreams are definitely symbolic. For example, maybe you've discovered the naked truth about a matter. If you're comfortable and not embarrassed by your nudity, the dream might mean that you're shedding an old role, represented by clothes, and becoming someone new.

Depending on how you feel about being nude, your dream might relate to anxiety—specifically something in your life that's being exposed. Or, it might relate to a wish for more exposure of something.

If you've dreamed of being nude in public, ask yourself these questions:

- ✪ What were you doing while you were nude?

- ✪ If other people are in the dream, how did they relate to your nudity?
- ✪ How did you feel about not wearing clothes?
- ✪ Are you keeping something under wraps that needs to be exposed?
- ✪ Can you relate the way you feel to anything going on in your life?

Teeth Falling Out

If you've lost your teeth in a dream, it may mean you need to visit the dentist, but it might mean something completely different. As symbols, teeth are related to strength, power, or aggressiveness, as in "sinking your teeth" into something. When teeth fall out in a dream, which is surprisingly common, the dream reflects a concern about weakness. Such dreams can also relate to an inability to communicate or to grasp a situation. Usually these dreams leave you feeling disturbed, but they don't create the fears and anxiety that a nightmare does.

If you've lost your teeth in a dream, ask yourself these questions:

- ✪ What's going on in the dream when you lose your teeth?
- ✪ Is someone else in the dream? If so, do you know the person? How does he or she relate to you losing your teeth?
- ✪ How did you feel about losing your teeth—panicked, upset, worried, resigned?
- ✪ Is there something in your life that's causing you to feel a loss of power or a sense of losing face?

Finding Money

If you dream of finding money, you can always hope it's a precognitive dream and you're about to discover a hidden cache! But chances are the dream was symbolic. Actually, a lot of people dream of finding money. As a teen, I used to dream of digging under the trunk of a large oak tree and finding piles of old coins. Such dreams usually suggest that you're searching for something of value or uncovering it. Discovering gold coins might indicate success in a matter at hand. Ancient coins could relate to some matter from the past that is coming to a head, probably in your favor.

If you've had a dream in which you've discovered money, ask yourself these questions:

- ✪ How did you feel when you made the discovery?
- ✪ What discoveries are you making or hope to make in your waking life?
- ✪ Do others value what you do?
- ✪ If you're finding coins, what do they look like?
- ✪ What did you do with the coins?

Water Dreams

Dreams about water are common, but not generic. Their meanings vary, depending on the circumstances of your dream. Stormy waters can relate to strong emotions. Floating comfortably in a pool offers a pleasant, weightless sensation. It might suggest that you may need to take a break from things that are burdening you.

Flowing water might indicate undercurrents in your life, or deep meanings related to the unconscious mind. If you're drowning in a dream, you need to look for a possible metaphor. Consider what conditions in your life leave you feeling as if you're over your head, or out of your depths, or simply drowning. If you're diving into water, you could be immersing yourself in something.

If you've had a dream involving water, ask yourself these questions:

- ⊗ How did you relate to the water? Were you floating on it, drowning in it, watching it, or going with the flow?
- ⊗ How did you feel about the water? Was it comforting, overwhelming, cold, powerful, calm, flowing, clear, or murky?
- ⊗ Can you relate your feelings about the water to anything taking place in your life?
- ⊗ Are there other people in the dream? If so, ask them what they're doing there. What is their purpose?

Finding a Bathroom

This dream might simply mean that you need to get up and go to the bathroom. Young children who wet beds often dream that they are in the bathroom instead of bed and are surprised when they wake up to a wet bed. If you're taking a shower in your dream, it might be symbolic of a need to clean up something in your life. Sometimes bathroom dreams are attention-getters as when you walk into a public bathroom and find both sexes. Such dreams might suggest a desire to break out of a mold or break a taboo.

If you've determined your dream isn't simply the call of nature, ask yourself these questions:

- ⊗ What's going on in your bathroom dream? Are you relieving yourself or are you taking a shower?
- ⊗ If it's a public bathroom, who else is present?
- ⊗ Is there something you need to eliminate or cleanse from your life? What's blocking you from doing so?
- ⊗ If someone else is in the bathroom, what does that person mean to you?
- ⊗ How did you feel when you woke up: anxious, relieved, cleansed?

Death Dreams

If you've dreamed of dying, you can relax. In all likelihood, it doesn't mean that you're going to die—at least not any time soon. In fact, most people who are about to die dream about their life, not their death. Dreaming of your death actually might mean that you are undergoing a transformation of some sort. It might involve moving to another town or city and changing schools. For a teen, it might relate to the transformation to adulthood, possibly triggered by graduating and leaving home for college.

Many dreams about death involve car crashes. In these cases, the car serves as a metaphor for where you're going in life and how the journey is unfolding.

In rare circumstances, death dreams are actually warnings. You might identify such dreams by their realistic details. If you dream of the brakes failing on your car, it could be a warning, rather than a symbol of feeling out of control. If the car looks exactly like your parents' car and other details, such as the highway and surroundings, are realistic, it's probably a good idea to take the dream seriously.

While the vast majority of death dreams are symbolic, as already mentioned, here are some questions you might ask if you have a dream about death and are concerned that it might be a warning:

- ✪ How realistic was the dream?
- ✪ Can you describe the details of the setting?
- ✪ Did you recognize other people in the dream? Did they look like they do in your waking life?
- ✪ Is there anything going on in your life that feels like the death dream scenario?
- ✪ If you're truly concerned that it might be a warning, is there anything you can do to prevent the dream scenario from becoming a reality?

Glossary

Bilocation — The alleged ability to be seen in two places at the same time.

Brain — The physical aspect of intelligence. Your brain is like a supercomputer with an enormous memory capacity. It processes information from your mind. (See Mind.)

Clairvoyance — Obtaining information about a person, place, object, or event at a distant location through psychic power. A French word that literally translates to "clear seeing." (See Remote viewing.)

Divination — Foretelling future events usually using tools or techniques such as reading tarot cards, I Ching coins, rune stones, tea leaves, or any other means of connecting the present with possible future events. Astrology is also considered a form of divination availing the stars and planets.

ESP — Short for extrasensory perception, the term was created by Dr. J. B. Rhine and refers to information gained through means beyond the five senses, usually telepathy, clairvoyance, and precognition.

Fire immunity — The ability to come into direct contact with extreme heat, such as fire or hot coals, without being burned.

Ghosts — Manifestations of energy, usually images of the deceased. Also described as consciousness without a body. Often the ghostly "performance" is repeated from time to time like a recording of past events. Some researchers believe ghosts are trapped spirits who haven't left the earth plane and are unaware they are no longer among the living. In rare cases, they appear related to malevolent entities.

Hauntings — Recurrent phenomena—apparitions, sounds, movement of objects, and other effects—reported to occur in particular locations.

Intuition — A general term for psychic functioning. Historically, it was thought of as a soft or unreliable form of information gathering and was associated with women. In contrast, men had hunches or gut feelings.

Levitation — The power to defy gravity, usually associated with psychic powers rather than normal forces of energy.

Metaphysics — In the traditional, philosophical sense, the pursuit of the underlying nature of reality. The popular meaning refers to the study of extrasensory perception and mysticism.

Mind — Your total intelligence. Your mind is not your brain. Rather, it directs information to you through your brain. Your mind isn't physical and never dies.

Mysticism — Experiences of unity with a higher awareness, the universe, or God; a sense of all things being related.

Near-death experience — An experience reported by those who have been revived from nearly dying. NDEs often involve feelings of peace, out-of-body sensations, seeing lights, and other phenomena.

New Age — A term related to the belief that mysticism can and should be applied to our everyday lives, and thus revealing a greater reality beyond the physical world.

OBE — Out-of-body experience; the experience of feeling separated from the body, often accompanied by visual perceptions as though from above the body.

Occult — Literally "the unknown," refers to the interest in or study of paranormal phenomena. It's often used as a disparaging term by those who fear or disapprove exploration of the paranormal and associate it with evil.

Paranormal — The realm of phenomena that exists beyond the material or physical world, or experiences with such phenomena.

Parapsychology — The scientific study of psychic phenomena. The best known parapsychologist was J. B. Rhine, who tested people for psychic abilities in the middle of the last century at Duke University. His work is being continued by others at the Rhine Institute for Parapsychology. Parapsychology is not the study of all things considered weird or bizarre. Nor is parapsychology concerned with astrology, UFOs, searching for Bigfoot, paganism, vampires, alchemy, or witchcraft.

Poltergeist — Recurring psychokinetic phenomena in which objects spontaneously fly about, fall, or move. While large-scale PK phenomena are often attributed to spirits, most researchers now associate the incidents with a living person, frequently an adolescent.

Precognition — Literally "to know in advance;" information about future events that is gained through psychic ability. Also called premonition.

Psi — A letter from the Greek alphabet that's used as a neutral term for ESP and psychokinetic phenomena.

Psychic — The ability to connect with an invisible reality through ESP, or a person who has such abilities.

Psychic power — Using psychic ability to enhance your awareness and improve your life.

Psychical research — A term that predates parapsychology, but also relates to the scientific study of ESP.

Psychokinesis — Direct mental influence on physical objects, animate or inanimate, without the use of known physical energies. Also called PK and telekinesis.

Psychometry — The ability to sense the history of an object by holding it. It's best known for its use by psychics in criminal investigations and archaeological research.

Reincarnation — The belief that we live successive lives, with primary evidence coming from the apparent recollections of previous lives by very small children.

Remote viewing — A term used by the U.S. military and intelligence agencies for clairvoyance, or the ability to gather information about a person, place, or object located at a distance from the viewer. It was practiced extensively in experiments in the 1980s and 1990s as a means of spying.

Retrocognition — Seeing into the past through the use of psychic ability, such as psychometry.

Spirits — The nonphysical aspect of deceased humans. Although sometimes associated with ghosts, spirits are usually considered beings on a higher plane, acting in a benevolent manner.

Subconscious — Below the level of the conscious mind, the part of the mind that links us to psychic experiences. You access your subconscious, and the psychic realm, through a shift of awareness.

Synchronicity — A meaningful coincidence, when two or more seemingly unrelated events come together, often in a striking fashion.

Telepathy — The ability to send and receive information through ESP, direct mind-to-mind communication.

Teleportation — A psychic ability related to psychokinesis in which objects are moved to distant locations.

Zener cards — ESP cards used for experiments. The deck of twenty-five cards features five symbols — star, wavy lines, square, circle, and cross—repeated five times.

Bibliography

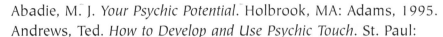

Abadie, M. J. *Your Psychic Potential.* Holbrook, MA: Adams, 1995.

Andrews, Ted. *How to Develop and Use Psychic Touch.* St. Paul: Llewellyn Publications, 1999.

Belitz, Charlene, and Meg Lundstrom. *The Power of Flow: Practical Ways to Transform Your Life with Meaningful Coincidence.* New York: Three Rivers Press, 1998.

Broughton, Richard S. *Parapsychology: The Controversial Science.* New York: Ballantine Books, 1991.

Brown, Sylvia. *Adventures of a Psychic.* Carlsbad, CA: Hay House, 1998.

Buhlman, William. *The Secret of the Soul.* San Francisco: Harper, 2001.

Combs, Allan, and Mark Holland. *Synchronicity: Science, Myth, and the Trickster.* New York: Paragon House, 1990.

Day, Laura. *Practical Intuition.* New York: Villard, 1996.

Einstein, Patricia. *Intuition: The Path to Inner Wisdom.* Rockport, MA: Element, 1997.

Gittelson, Bernard. *Intangible Evidence: Explore the World of Psychic Phenomena and Learn to Develop Your Psychic Skills.* New York: Fireside, 1987.

Guiley, Rosemary Ellen. *Dreamwork for the South: A Spiritual Guide to Dream Interpretation.* New York: Berkley, 1998.

Hamilton-Parker, Craig. *The Psychic Workbook.* London: Random House, 1995.

Heath, Pamela Rae. *The PK Zone: A Cross-Cultural Review of Psychokinesis (PK).* Nebraska: Universe, 2003.

Hewitt, William W. *Psychic Development for Beginners.* St. Paul: Llewellyn Publications, 2001.

Hoffman, Enid. *Develop Your Psychic Skills.* Rockport, MA: Para Research, 1981.

Hopcke, Robert H. *There Are No Accidents: Synchronicity and the Stories of Our Lives.* New York: Riverhead Books, 1997.

Koestler, Arthur. *The Roots of Coincidence*. New York: Random House, 1973.

LaBerge, Stephen, and Howard Rheingod. *Exploring the World of Lucid Dreaming*. New York: Ballantine, 1990.

MacGregor, Rob. *Dream Power for Teens*. Holbrook, MA: Adams, 2004.

MacGregor, Rob, and Trish MacGregor. *The Everything Dreams Book*. Holbrook, MA: Adams, 1997.

McElroy, Susan Chernak. *Animals as Teachers & Healers*. New York: Ballantine, 1997.

McMoneagle, Joseph. *Remote Viewing Secrets*. Charlottesville, VA: Hampton Roads, 2000.

———. *The Stargate Chronicles: Memoirs of a Psychic Spy*. Charlottesville, VA: Hampton Roads, 2002.

Mishlove, Jeffrey. *The PK Man: A True Story of Mind Over Matter*. Charlottesville, VA: Hampton Roads, 2000.

———. *The Roots of Consciousness: Psychic Liberation Through History, Science and Experience*. New York: Random House, 1975.

Monroe, Robert. *Journeys Out of Body*. New York: Anchor Books, 1971.

Moss, Robert. *Conscious Dreaming: A Spiritual Path for Everyday Life*. New York: Three Rivers Press, 1996.

Orloff, Judith, M.D. *Second Sight*. New York: Warner, 1996.

Peat, F. David. *Synchronicity: The Bridge Between Matter and Mind*. New York: Bantam, 1987.

Radin, Dean. *The Conscious Universe: The Scientific Truth of Psychic Phenomena*. San Francisco: Harper, 1997.

Sanders, Pete A., Jr. *You Are Psychic!* New York: Fawcett Columbine, 1989.

Sheldrake, Rupert. *Dogs That Know When Their Owners Are Coming Home*. New York: Random House, 1999.

———. *The Sense of Being Stared At...And Other Unexplained Powers of the Human Mind*. New York: Three Rivers Press, 2003.

Talbot, Michael. *Beyond the Quantum: How the Secrets of the New Physics Are Bridging the Chasm Between Science and Faith*. New York: Bantam, 1986.

———. *The Holographic Universe*. New York: HarperCollins, 1991.

Targ, Russell, and Jane Katra. *Miracles of the Mind*. Novta, CA: New World Library, 1998.

Targ, Russell, and Harold Puthoff. *Mind-Reach: Scientists Look at Psychic Ability*. New York: Delta Books, 1977.

Vaughan, Frances E. *Awakening Intuition*. New York: Anchor Books, 1979.

Webster, Richard. *Is Your Pet Psychic?* St. Paul: Llewellyn Publications, 2002.

Wesselman, Hank. *The Journey to the Sacred Garden, A Guide to Traveling in the Spiritual Realms*. Carlsbad, CA: Hay House, 2003.

Wilson, Colin. *The Supernatural*. New York: Carroll and Graf Publishers, 1991.